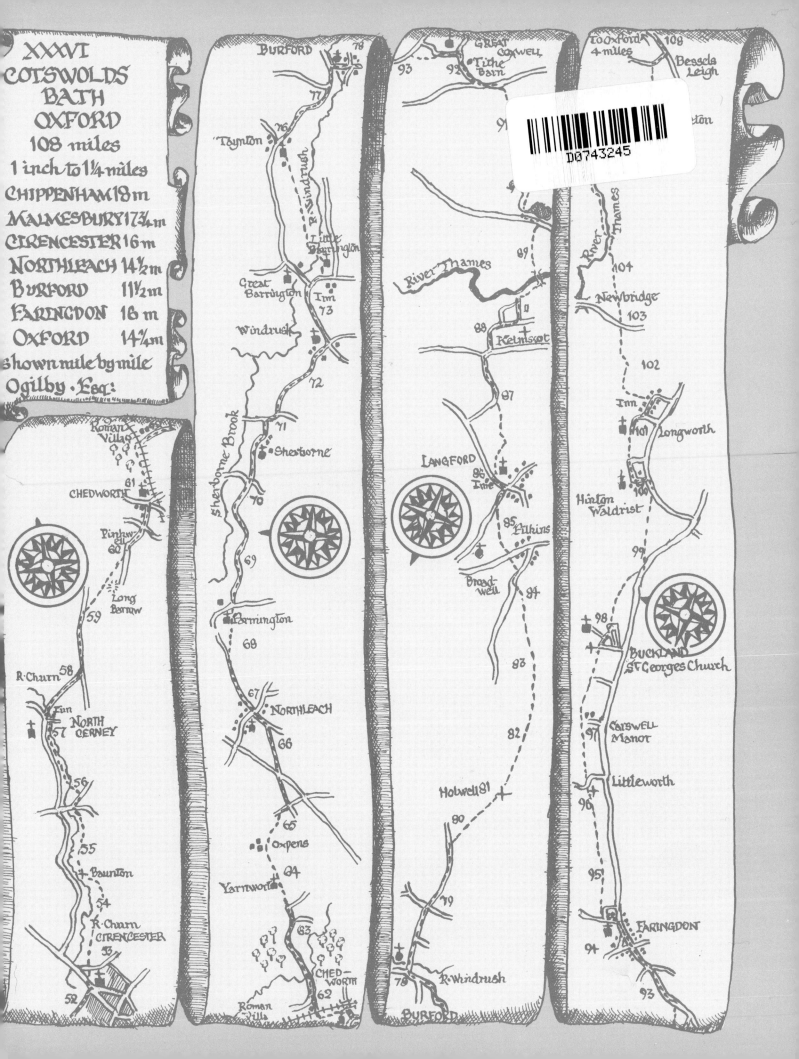

THE
WAYFARERS' JOURNAL

THE SPRING WALK

We had a pleasant walk to-day
Over the hills and far away.
Across the bridge by the water-mill
By the woodside and up the hill.
And if you listen to what I say
I'll tell you what we saw to-day.

The Wayfarers' Journal

A PILGRIMAGE THROUGH THE ENGLISH COUNTRYSIDE

Ashwell Church and Village.

JOHN LLOYD & PAT SELLARS

Introduction by Douglas McCreath

Webb & Bower

First published in Great Britain 1991 by Webb and Bower (Publishers) Limited 5 Cathedral Close, Exeter, Devon EX1 1EZ

Distributed by the Penguin Group Penguin Books Ltd, Registered Offices: Harmondsworth Middlesex, England
Penguin Books Australia Ltd, Ringwood, Victoria, Australia
Penguin Books Canada Ltd, 2801 John Stret, Markham, Ontario, Canada L3R 1B4
Penguin Books (NZ) Ltd, 182-190 Wairau Road, Auckland 10, New Zealand

Designed by Peter Wrigley

British Library Cataloguing in Publication Data

The Wayfarers journal : a pilgrimage through the English countryside.
1. England. Description & travel
I. McCreath, Douglas
914.204859

ISBN 0-86350-431-0

Typeset in Great Britain by P&M Typesetting Ltd, Exeter, Devon

Text set in Trajanus

Colour reproduction by Peninsular Repro Service Ltd, Exeter

Printed and bound in Great Britain by BPCC Hazell Books,
Aylesbury and Paulton

FRONTISPIECE
The verse 'The Spring Walk' is by Thomas Miller (1807-1874).
The illumination was inspired by a Book of Hours (of prayer)
seen in the church of SS. Peter and Paul, Swaffham (see p 39)

Contents

*The volume numbers and walk (ITER) numbers
are from the original work 'A Book of Walks'*

Hartfield.
Lych Gate

INTRODUCTION

IT WAS SHEER COINCIDENCE that brought what is now known as *The Wayfarers' Journal* to my attention. On a dull, wet day in April 1989 I was driving home to Glasgow from a business trip to the North-East of England when I pulled into the pub annexed to The George Hotel at Chollerford in Northumberland for a bite of lunch. The small bar was packed but a rather unkempt man made a space for me on his pew bench and I squeezed in next to him. For a while there was no conversation between us, he being contentedly immersed in his beer, me happily likewise in *The Times*; but eventually the ice broke and he told me that he was on a walking holiday, journeying along the length of Hadrian's Wall with some friends. The latter five men were sitting in companionable silence at a nearby table and my more talkative neighbour soon had me engrossed in tales of walks they had been making together over a long period; the first one, over thirty-five years ago had included himself and two others present in the bar. As he spoke it was impossible not to notice certain foibles about the group as a whole. None of them had shaved for some days and their garb, though sensible, owed nothing to designer fashion! Assorted hats and a variety of walking sticks lay scattered about and as each finished his drink he would rise and re-order only for himself. They seemed more content in their own company, and despite my stilted attempts at conversation they preserved their anonymity.

A Smoke and Tiffin in Apple orchards.

Red Lion - Horderley.

Later, almost casually, someone mentioned how they kept a record of all their travels in the form of illuminated manuscripts bound into a 'Book of Walks', and the two responsible for the calligraphy, text and illustrations were eventually persuaded to tell me about their craft. They seemed surprised at my interest in what they dismissed merely as 'a hobby', but I was fascinated with their descriptions of the medieval illuminations created for these mysterious diaries. It all sounded too good to be true and to satisfy my curiosity I asked if a photocopied page could be sent to me. Reaction among the group was muted, and guarded against my apparent invasion of privacy, but following some discussion they decided to hold an 'extraordinary meeting' and I was asked to move out of earshot – the jury was out! Soon the verdict was announced. To my relief I had won my appeal, and for payment of one pound sterling they would honour my request. By this time my day's schedule had fallen a long way behind, so with hurried apologies I paid my dues, bade farewell to the six (still anonymous) gentlemen and continued the journey north, my thoughts preoccupied with these eccentric characters. Unknowingly I had met John Lloyd, Pat Sellars and the Viatores.

Several weeks passed before the promised photocopy arrived in a carefully handscripted envelope. A short covering letter was signed 'John Lloyd, Scribe to the Viatores' and the enclosed exquisitely illuminated page told of a walk along part of the Suffolk coast, of birds, sea shells and Sizewell among other things. A curious and highly unusual presentation of life today in archaic form. I was captivated, and in the hope of learning more about the walkers and their 'Book of Walks' I embarked on what was to become regular correspondence with John Lloyd. Gradually over a period of months, the story unfolded.

It all began in 1953 when John Lloyd and Pat Sellars, then employed at British Telecom's headquarters in London discovered they shared interests in parish churches and similar antiquities in England, and they also enjoyed walking. Inspired by Hilaire Belloc's *The Old Road* they set out that year, accompanied by another acquaintance, H Valentine, to complete 'The Pilgrims Way' from Winchester to Canterbury, a distance of 112 miles, in seven days. Half-way along they were joined by Pat's brother Mick, and this walk founded a tradition still carried on to this day. Initially one a year was organized, subsequently two, but in the early years no attempt was made to keep a record of their journeyings. However, upon the death in 1960 of 'Val' it was decided that volumes should be produced covering each five-year period and this task fell to John and Pat. John (as Scribe) had already acquired considerable skill as a self-taught calligrapher and illuminator. He was familiar with medieval manuscripts and could reproduce original designs in initial letters and borders. Pat (as Author) was able to exercise his literary talents and would carefully check and research the mass of detail collected on each walk before passing the text to John. By 1990 they had completed five volumes and a sixth was in preparation covering walks up to 1983. These volumes were produced solely for the amusement and satisfaction of this little group of walkers and were certainly not intended for public view – in fact very few people had ever set eyes upon them. But I was lucky, because just when my hope was ebbing John, recognizing my genuine interest, invited me to London to see the originals.

My greatest expectations were more than realized. Five leather-bound and gold-tooled volumes consisting of page after sumptuous page of magnificent illustrations, gloriously colourful illuminations and beautifully constructed text all written on hand-made paper, lay before me. The binding was done by Bill Ward a member of the group and bookbinder by trade. John told me more about the group. Calling themselves the Viatores (Latin for 'the travellers') and taking the form of a confraternity they now consist of six full and two non-walking members (see Acknowledgements) plus an Honorary

Chaplain. They have a set of rules too – known as Guidelines – which instructs for example that 'Hats shall be worn for carrying Pilgrim badges and feathers', 'No member shall shave for the duration of a Walk' and 'Capes and Leggings shall be put on only when the Senior Member decrees a state of rain'! Another declares that tea must be brewed each afternoon, this being taken alfresco regardless of weather conditions. They must not wear clothing of an outrageous nature nor buy drinks for one another and walking sticks shall be carried. Thus Chollerford was explained! Rule 19 ominously declares "Members shall consciously avoid contact with the Media on pain of punishment"… could perhaps an exception be made in this case?

The outstanding quality of these books, and the interesting characters behind them, convinced me that the volumes should be published, though this ambition would not easily be fulfilled. The work was never intended for wider circulation and quite naturally there was initial apprehension among the members, but when eventually permission came, I had no difficulty in finding a supportive publisher in Richard Webb. The extracts in this unique presentation are a glowing testimony to the participants' good humoured respect, love and knowledge of our historic countryside.

DOUGLAS McCREATH
Drymen
Stirlingshire
1990

n the eighteenth of Sept~ember 1953 we set out from Winchester to walk to Canterbury. This was the first of a long series of walks in the South Country undertaken usually by the four of us either in Spring or Autumn. This book is a simple record of the places we saw; but though it is little more than a log-book, it seeks to make permanent the fleeting joys of travel on foot. These joys are to us very real but they appear to escape most of our fellows for we seldom meet others who walk all day for pleasure. As we tread with stout staff the green roads of England there comes upon us at times the feeling that we are walking anachronisms, that life has passed us by ~ on wheels; but, like Belloc, we would take advantage of no wheeled thing unless we were benighted or the journey at an end. The pity is that each journey has to end for we travel hoping never to arrive. Thus we like best a walk of several days because the end is never in sight until the last day. We observe more or less a few simple rules. These are first that no-one shall wear boots lest he have an unfair advantage in deep mud, secondly that a halt shall be called every hour for a long as is necess-ary to stand and stare back at the country behind us and thirdly that a midday meal of bread cheese and beer shall be taken. As the morale of the party is so dependent upon it, this last rule is scrupulously obs-erved despite the fact that finding an inn between certain variable hours makes such exacting demands upon the navigator who long ago gave up the practice of arranging for an afternoon cup of tea as well さ さ さ

One final rule to be observed is that the going shall be soft and that therefore the metalled road is the last resort. In these days roads divide the country into 'insulae' as did the streets of Roman towns. Motorists glimpse the country through the windows of their mobiles detachable-rooms and know little of it in consequence. To enter an insula from the boundary road is to make a voyage of discovery usually along a footpath neglected in favour of the motor bus or car. Within each insula we enjoy every blade of grass as we walk among the untrodden ways. There, within the insula, we reach our objective – the English scene. The moving camera of the eye records it and the mind delights in it; it is better than television. We have become acutely aware that in the English scene we have inherited a glorious collection of parkland, museum, garden, natural scenery and skyscape which is daily threatened on all sides by unsightly development. We traverse the country rejoicing where modern development is tasteful or, better still, absent. We are thankful that we can still dwell upon beauty and have not lost the capacity to wonder. It is also a recurring wonder to us that we are able to get away for a few days each year and that those few days should coincide. For this annual miracle we have our wives to thank. Without their co-operation this book would never have appeared; we dedicate it to them.

Val – Stanmore, Middlesex   ✛   Pat – Bracknell, Berks
John – Caterham, Surrey   ✛   Mick – Southampton, Hants

EASTWARDS·WENT
from Winchester in
nineteen fifty three,
Masters Sellars,
Lloyd and Valentine,
Civil Servants three. Through the southron Counties the modern pilgrims strode, Receiving somewhat tardily "the spirit of the road". No beast
of burden had they and on their backs they bore,
The minimum necessities but very little more.
With Belloc's inspiration and his "Old Road" their
guide, From way of ancient pilgrims they scarcely
turned aside. They climbed and dipped and forded
for seven days and nights, Till reaching Canterbury gates they met a goodly sight, Robed Church-
men with their acolytes on penitential mile,
Bearing this martyr's relic in reverent meas-
ured file.

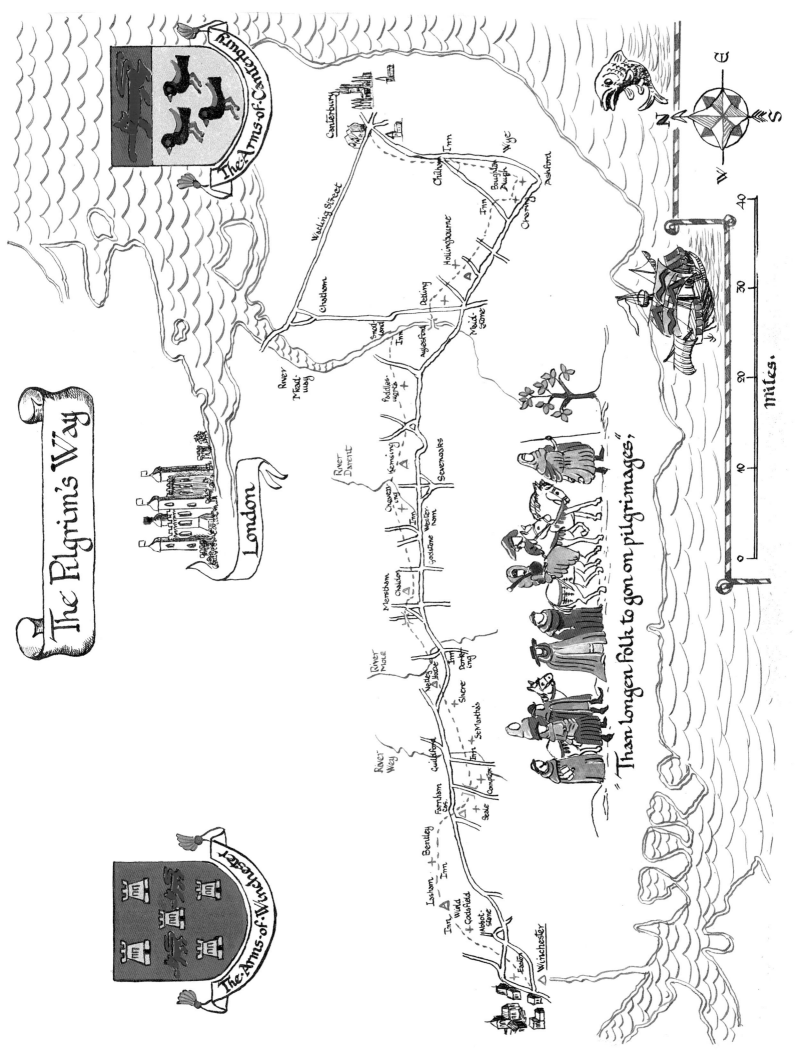

OCTOBER · 1956 ·
AND · AS · A · MAN · WILL
paint with a peculiar passion
a face which he is only per-
mitted to see for a little time,
so will one passionately
set down one's own horizon
and one's fields before they are forgotten and
have become a different thing. Therefore it is that I have put down in writing
what happened to me now so many years ago,
when I met first one man and then another, and
we four bound ourselves together and walked
through all your land, Sussex, from end to end.
For many years I have meant to write it down
and have not; nor would I write it down now,
Sussex, did I not know that you, who must like
all created things decay, might with the rest
of us be very near your ending.
Hilaire Belloc ·   The Four Men.

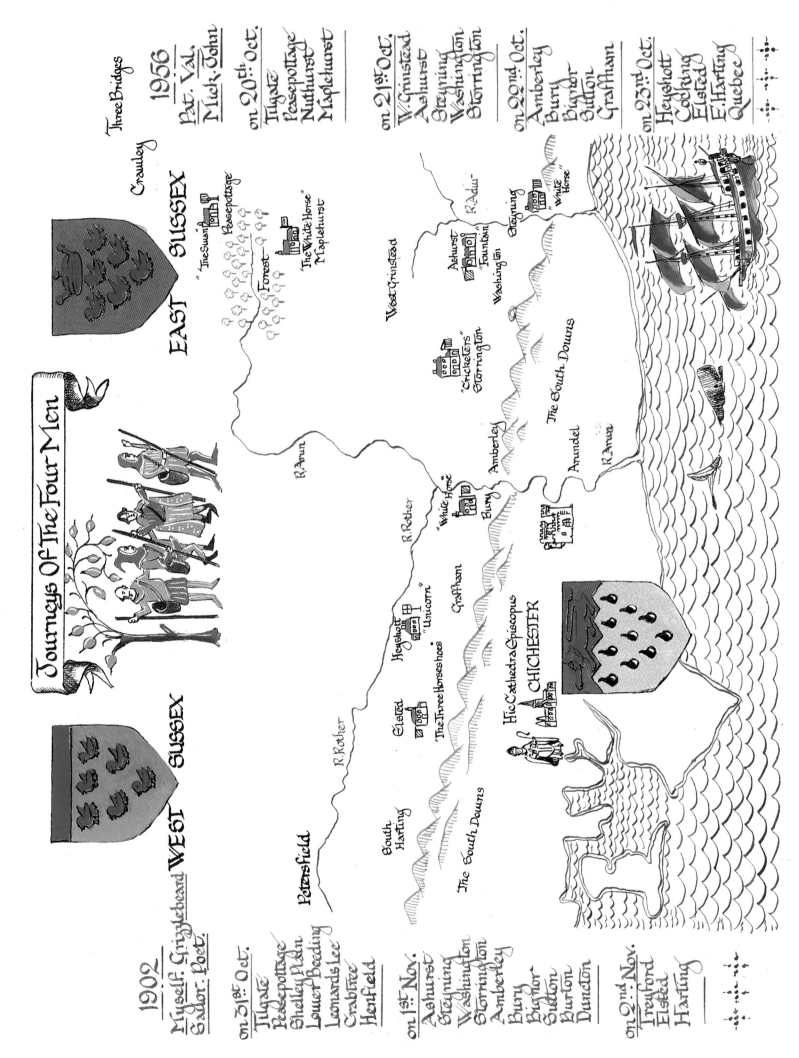

Journeys Of The Four Men

Three Bridges

1956

<u>Pat. Val.</u>
<u>Mich. John</u>

on 20th. Oct.
<u>Tilgate</u>
Peasepottage
Nuthurst
Maplehurst

on 21st. Oct.
<u>W. Grinstead</u>
Ashurst
Steyning
Washington
Storrington

on 22nd. Oct.
<u>Amberley</u>
Bury
Bignor
Sutton
Graffham

on 23rd. Oct.
<u>Heyshott</u>
Cocking
Elsted
E. Harting
Quebec

Crawley

EAST SUSSEX

"The Swan" Peasepottage

Forest

"The White Horse" Maplehurst

West Grinstead

R. Adur

Ashurst "Fountain" Steyning

Washington

"White Horse"

"Cricketers" Storrington

The South Downs

Amberley

Arundel

R. Arun

R. Arun

R. Rother

"White Horse"
Bury

Graffham

Heyshott "Unicorn"

Elsted
"The Three Horseshoes"

The South Downs

Hic Cathedra Episcopus
CHICHESTER

South Harting

Petersfield

R. Rother

The South Downs

1902

<u>Myself. Grizzlebeard</u>
<u>Sailor. Poet.</u>

on 31st. Oct.
<u>Tilgate</u>
Peasepottage
Shelley Plain
Lower Beeding
Leonardslee
Crabtree
Henfield

on 1st. Nov.
<u>Ashurst</u>
Steyning
Washington
Storrington
Amberley
Bury
Bignor
Sutton
Burton
Duncton

on 2nd. Nov.
<u>Treyford</u>
Elsted
Harting

WEST SUSSEX

URING THE PAST FIVE YEARS when we walked together once and sometimes twice a year, there grew up between us a bond of friendship which generally lay dormant but which came to life as each new walk began ~ because friendship is usually about something and ours is concerned with walking. A mountaineer suffering from frostbite was asked by Bishop John Hughes of Croydon why he went climbing. He replied that there were three motives - the companionship, the beauty and to know himself. We too had discovered that companionship is necessary for the fullest appreciation of beauty and that when beauty was absent from built-up areas or dull country, companionship consoled us. With C·S·Lewis we felt lucky beyond desert to be in such company. Especially when the whole group is together each bringing out all that is best, wisest or funniest in all the others. Those are the golden sessions when four of us after a hard day's walking have come to our inn; when our slippers are on, our feet spread out towards the blaze and our drinks at our elbows; when the whole world and something beyond the world opens itself to our minds as we talk and no-one has any claim on or responsibility for another, but all are freemen and equals as if we had first met an hour ago, while at the same time an affection mellowed by the years enfolds us. Life ~ natural life ~ has no better gift to give. Who could have deserved it? Possibly we have not yet learned to know ourselves as the mountaineer had done. Certainly we were aware that these pleasures would pass one day and that we could not expect to remain together to the end. Uneasily we had noticed that Val was failing and might not remain with us much longer. One day we would each have to learn that "there is one road none may travel but thou only".

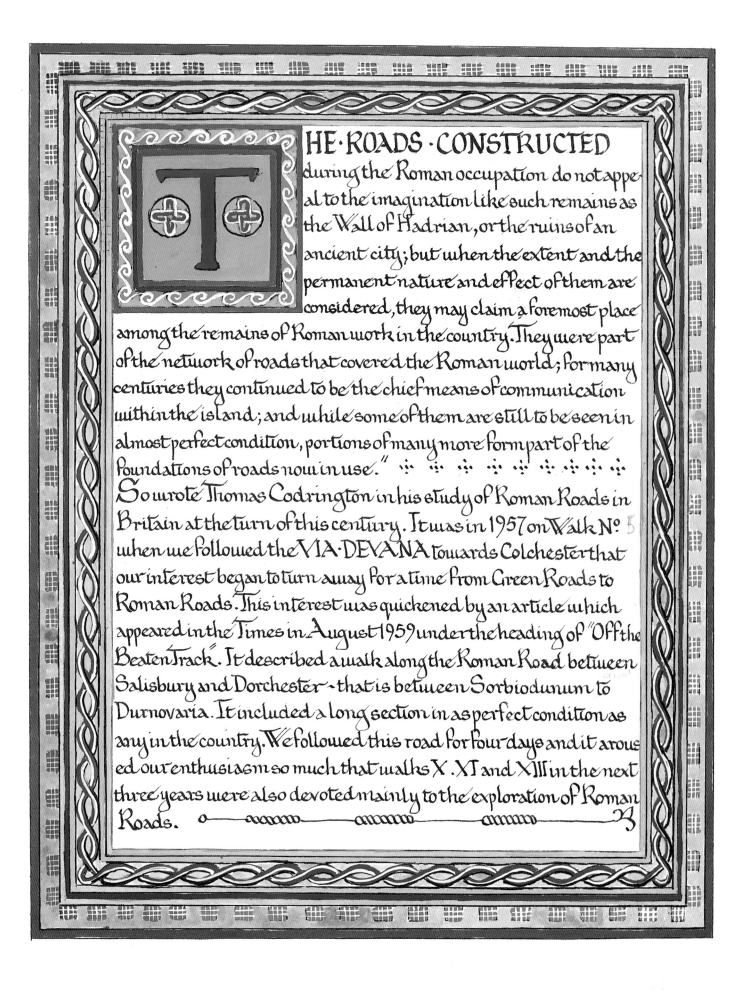

"HE·ROADS·CONSTRUCTED during the Roman occupation do not appeal to the imagination like such remains as the Wall of Hadrian, or the ruins of an ancient city; but when the extent and the permanent nature and effect of them are considered, they may claim a foremost place among the remains of Roman work in the country. They were part of the network of roads that covered the Roman world; for many centuries they continued to be the chief means of communication within the island; and while some of them are still to be seen in almost perfect condition, portions of many more form part of the foundations of roads now in use."

So wrote Thomas Codrington in his study of Roman Roads in Britain at the turn of this century. It was in 1957 on Walk No. 5 when we followed the VIA·DEVANA towards Colchester that our interest began to turn away for a time from Green Roads to Roman Roads. This interest was quickened by an article which appeared in the Times in August 1959 under the heading of "Off the Beaten Track". It described a walk along the Roman Road between Salisbury and Dorchester—that is between Sorbiodunum to Durnovaria. It included a long section in as perfect condition as any in the country. We followed this road for four days and it aroused our enthusiasm so much that walks X, XI and XIII in the next three years were also devoted mainly to the exploration of Roman Roads.

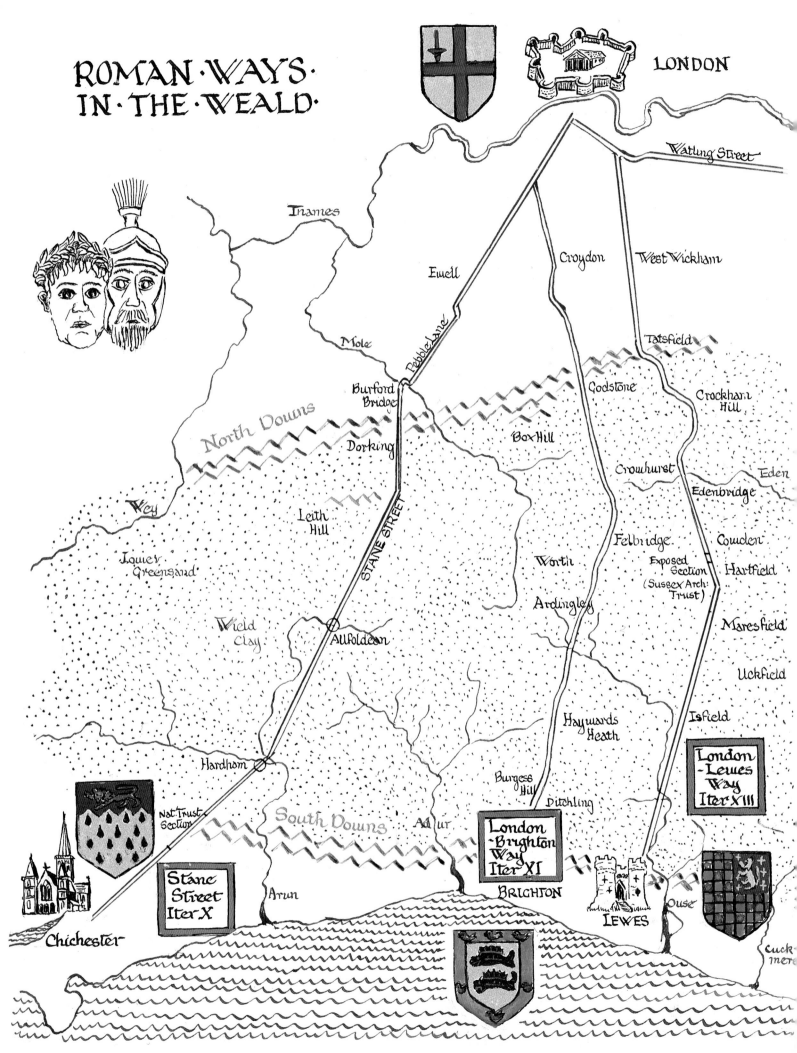

ROMAN·WAYS·
IN·THE·WEALD·

LONDON

Watling Street

Thames

Ewell

Croydon

West Wickham

Pebble Lane

Mole

Tatsfield

Burford Bridge

North Downs

Godstone

Crockham Hill

Dorking

Box Hill

Crowhurst

Eden

Edenbridge

Wey

Leith Hill

STANE STREET

Cowden

Felbridge

Exposed Section (Sussex Arch: Trust)

Hartfield

Lower Greensand

Worth

Weald Clay

Ardingley

Maresfield

Alfoldean

Uckfield

Hardham

Nat. Trust Section

Haywards Heath

Isfield

South Downs

Burgess Hill

Ditchling

Adur

London -Lewes Way Iter XIII

Stane Street Iter X

London -Brighton Way Iter XI

BRIGHTON

LEWES

Chichester

Arun

Ouse

Cuckmere

Some luck is needed
You may walk
that way a
hundred times
And then
In a certain light
And at the right season,
Say when the smallest
shoots
Best show the shaping
of the soil

Like some close-fitting coat,
Then you may see the line
Across that lonely field
And looking where their
road once went
You see the Roman might
Just like a blaze of
distant light~
And brighter still for all
the dark between

Bernard Berry

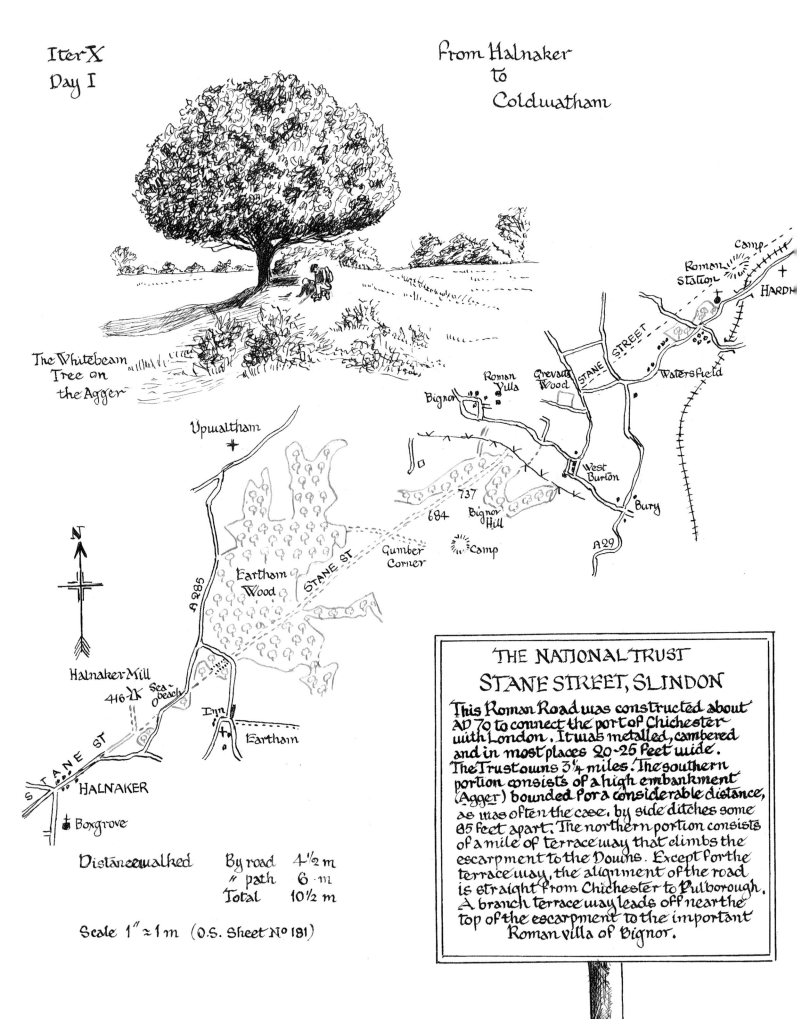

Iter X
Day I

from Halnaker
to
Coldwatham

The Whitebeam
Tree on
the Agger

Camp.
Roman
Station
HARDH

STANE STREET

Grevatt Wood
Watersfield

Roman Villa
Bignor

Upwaltham

West Burton

737
684   Bignor Hill

Bury

A29

Camp

N

Gumber Corner

Eartham Wood

STANE ST

A 285

STANE ST

Halnaker Mill
416
Sea-
beach

Inn
Eartham

HALNAKER

Boxgrove

Distance walked   By road   4½ m
                    " path   6 m
                   Total   10½ m

Scale 1" ≈ 1 m (O.S. Sheet Nº 181)

THE NATIONAL TRUST
STANE STREET, SLINDON

This Roman Road was constructed about
AD 70 to connect the port of Chichester
with London. It was metalled, cambered
and in most places 20-25 feet wide.
The Trust owns 3¼ miles. The southern
portion consists of a high embankment
(Agger) bounded for a considerable distance,
as was often the case, by side ditches some
85 feet apart. The northern portion consists
of a mile of terrace way that climbs the
escarpment to the Downs. Except for the
terrace way, the alignment of the road
is straight from Chichester to Pulborough.
A branch terrace way leads off near the
top of the escarpment to the important
Roman villa of Bignor.

The Stane Street   Iter X

From Halnaker to Hardham   *Saturday 11th February 1961*

e had decided to walk up Stane Street from Chichester to Dorking but, having only two days free, we used buses to cover those sections still in use as motor-roads. Our first bus took us to Halnaker where we had walked a short section of Stane Street in the previous autumn. The first alignment from Chichester, on a bearing of 62°, goes towards Pulborough well away from the direction of London. This avoids Leith Hill and also a steep descent of the South Downs. Leaving the main road at Seabeach we found the agger in an open beechwood and then turned off to find once again the George and Dragon at Eartham where we were joined for lunch by a fine boxer dog. Rejoining the line of Stane Street where we had left it, we walked up the sector owned by the National Trust and soon came on the lone tree on the agger, recorded in Iter IX as a hornbeam. A specimen leaf from it was since identified by the Royal Botanic Gardens, Kew as that of a White Beam "frequent on calcareous soils especially in the south". We came near this crest of the downs to the wide common of yew and hawthorn and as the round top of Bignor Hill came into sight there was the signpost pointing back to "REGNUM". This recalled our earlier discussion about the correct name for Chichester. The name Noviomagus Regnenses is given in the Ordnance Survey Map of Roman Britain and seems to have been a combination of the new Roman city and the old capital Regnum of the tribe called Regnenses.

On the left of the lane going downhill from Gumber Corner we saw the terrace way which we had missed last autumn and also the short branch terrace leading from it to the villa at Bignor. From the corner of Bignortail Wood at the foot of the downs we used Mick's copy of "Roman Ways in the Weald" to follow hedgerows and woods northwards and look for some sign of the Roman watering trough in Grevatt's wood. Finally with the light beginning to fail before five o-clock we abandoned the true alignment at Watersfield. Had there been more time available to us, we would have gone to find the first of the "mansiones" or posting-stations at Hardham. This was a small rectangular and embanked enclosure serving, like a coaching inn, the needs of travellers at the end of their first day from Chichester. The second posting-station is at Alfoldean some twelve miles on, a little smaller than Hardham and with a bridge across the Arun where wooden piles, now in Lewes museum, were found in recent years. As that part of Stane Street between Hardham and Alfoldean was nearly all main road, we took a bus to our own posting-station at Horsham.

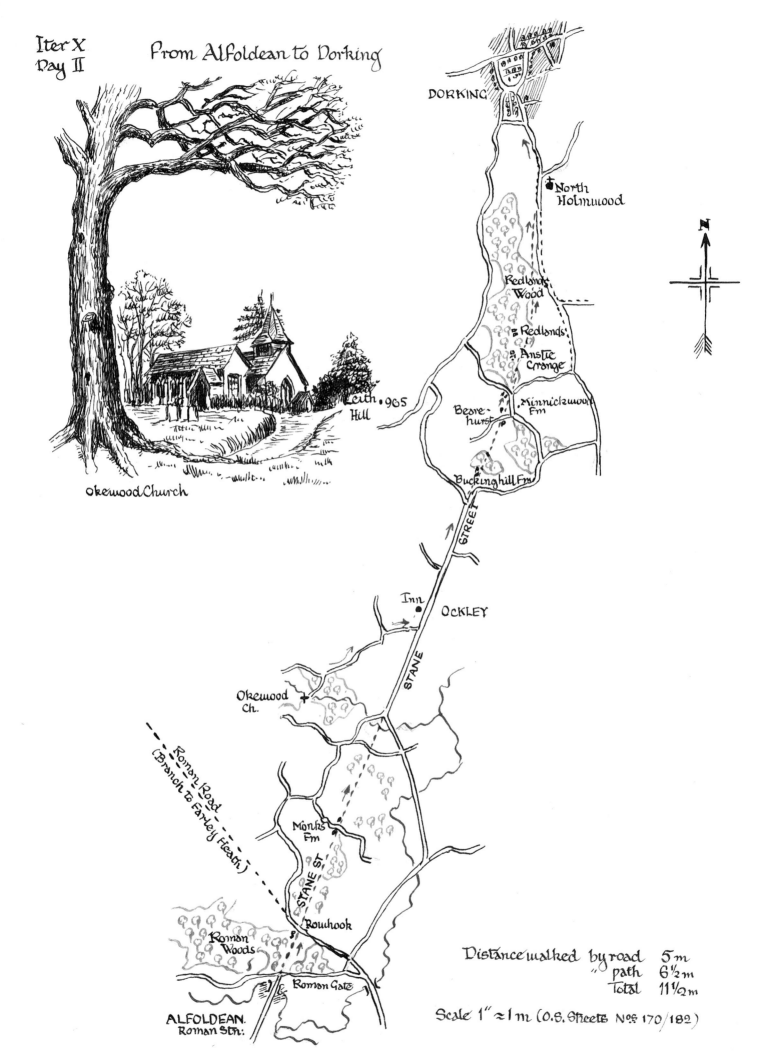

Iter X
Day II

From Alfoldean to Dorking

DORKING

North Holmwood

Redlands Wood

Redlands

Anstie Grange

Minnickwood Fm

Beare hurst

Buckinghill Fm

GREET

Inn   OCKLEY

STANE

Okewood Ch.

Roman Road
(Branch to Farley Heath)

Monks Fm

STANE ST.

Rowhook

Roman Woods

Roman Gate

ALFOLDEAN.
Roman Stn:

Okewood Church

Leith · 965
Hill

Distance walked by road   5 m
       "   path   6½ m
                Total 11½ m

Scale 1" ≈ 1 m (O.S. Sheets Nºs 170/182)

Alfoldean to Dorking   *Sunday 12th February 1961*

A fter a short bus journey from Horsham we rejoined the line of Stane Street at Roman Gate close to the second posting-station. The third station is assumed to be at Dorking though it has never been located. Thus our journey today, like that of yesterday, was a typical day's march between two mansions as in Roman times. It began well with a climb through Roman Woods on the prolongation of that long alignment from Pulborough on the A29 which points accurately to London Bridge. We crossed a lane at Rowhook whence runs a small branch Roman road towards a Roman temple at Farley Heath. In the next two miles, the course of Stane Street could easily be followed by the hedgerows on a parish boundary, edges of woods and occasional tracks. This part of the road did not have the dramatic quality of Ackling Dyke or the sector up to Gumber Corner but it was nonetheless a pleasure to follow and there were no serious obstacles. A few primroses on banks under the oaks gave added pleasure. At Okewoodhill where there is a kink in the road designed to avoid a steep-sided ghyll we branched off to the west to see Okewood church. There it stood on its little knoll deep among oak and hazel woods and approached only by means of stone flagged paths and a lane ending at the church. Great Horsham Slabs covered the roof and the walls were heavily buttressed. Except for the 'de la Hale' brass in the old chancel floor it was not a church of great interest but its setting was quite lovely. We had lunch in a small inn full of Sunday walkers in Ockley. Mick's map of Surrey dated 1805 gives the name Stane Street for the two miles of raised causeway forming the main road through the village. With the long broad green on one side, this road through Ockley is a fine sight. At the north end of the causeway Mick took a forward bearing towards Buckinghill Farm as the Roman Road once more disappeared into a series of woods, private grounds and small parks. In these last four miles to Dorking the road, whose direction had not changed for so many miles, altered course twice. First at Bearehurst there was a slight change of a few degrees to the east to avoid a spur from Leith Hill and then came a 20° turn to the west to enable the road to pass through the Downs by the River Mole gap. We plunged on hopefully, off course for most of the time. We even failed to see the terrace in Redlands Wood which was turfed over in 1935 to preserve it. When finally we entered Dorking and sat over fish and chips in the centre of the town we wished we had a third day free to go on to the next posting-station over the Mickleham Downs to Ewell. We also wondered if there were any truth in the story that Billingshurst and Billingsgate were both named after Belinus the builder of Stane Street.

The End of the Tenth Walk

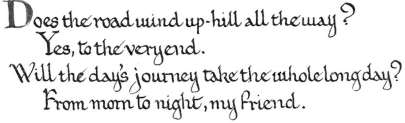

Does the road wind up-hill all the way?
	Yes, to the very end.
Will the day's journey take the whole long day?
	From morn to night, my friend.

But is there for the night a resting place?
	A roof for when the slow dark hours begin
May not the darkness hide it from my face?
	You cannot miss that inn.

Shall I meet other wayfarers at night?
	Those who have gone before.
Then must I knock, or call when just in sight?
	They will not keep you standing at that door

Shall I find comfort, travel-sore and weak?
	Of labour you shall find the sum.
Will there be beds for me and all who seek?
	Yea, beds for all who come.

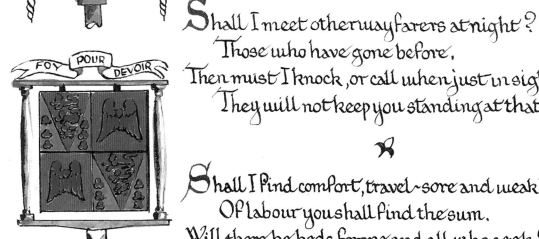

Christina Rossetti

Wiltshire Trackways

The map is drawn around the western part of Salisbury Plain and shows features existing more than a thousand years ago ~ trackways, earthworks, hill-forts and rivers. A few modern place-names connecting our route are also shown. ⁜ ⁜ ⁜ ⁜

In the extreme west on the Somerset border the Plain is broken into many separate hills. Here, whence rivers may flow either to the English Channel or the Bristol Channel, is a nodal point for the great chalk ridges of the South. Here also the two greatest and most ancient trackways intersect. One is the Great Ridgeway, the prehistoric highway from East Anglia to Devon (see Walks VII and XX). The other is called the Harrow Way and it goes eastwards along the foot of the North Downs (see Walks I and II)

In the Spring of 1962 we followed some of the main watersheds where such ancient track-ways go. We saw the old settlements, burial places and earthworks or hill-forts along the trackways. It was splendid open downland, clear and dry in the stiff winds of March. At midday and nightfall and some other times we came down to the villages to seek food and shelter or visit a church. And always there was a welcom-ing inn with beds for all who come. ⁜

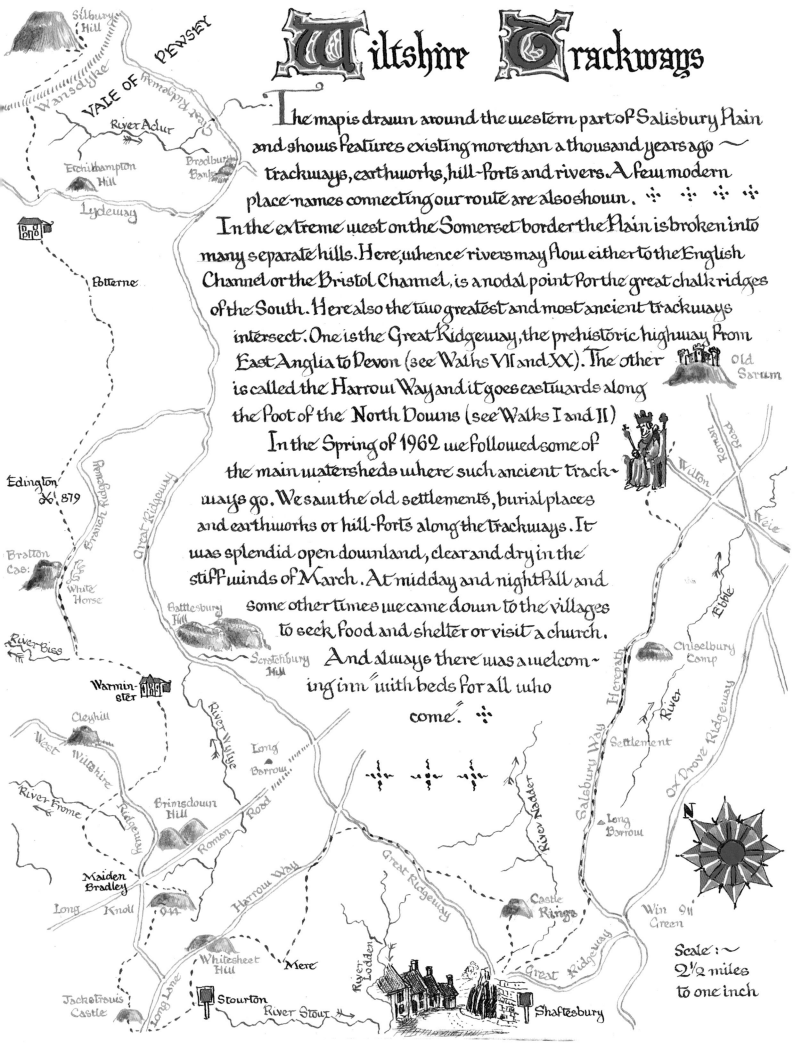

Silbury Hill
Wansdyke
VALE OF PEWSEY
Great Ridgeway
River Adur
Etchilhampton Hill
Bradbury Banks
Lydeway
Potterne
Edington 879
Branch Ridgeway
Great Ridgeway
Bratton Cas.
White Horse
River Biss
Battlesbury Hill
Scratchbury Hill
Warminster
Cley Hill
West Wiltshire Ridgeway
River Frome
Brimsdown Hill
River Wylye
Long Barrow
Roman Road
Maiden Bradley
Long Knoll
944
Harrow Way
Whitesheet Hill
Long Lane
Jack Straw's Castle
Stourton
Mere
River Stour
River Lodden
Old Sarum
Wilton
Roman Road
Wye
Ebble
Chiselbury Camp
Herepath
River
Salisbury Way
Settlement
Ox Drove Ridgeway
Long Barrow
River Nadder
Great Ridgeway
Castle Rings
Win Green 911
Great Ridgeway
Shaftesbury

N

Scale :~
2½ miles
to one inch

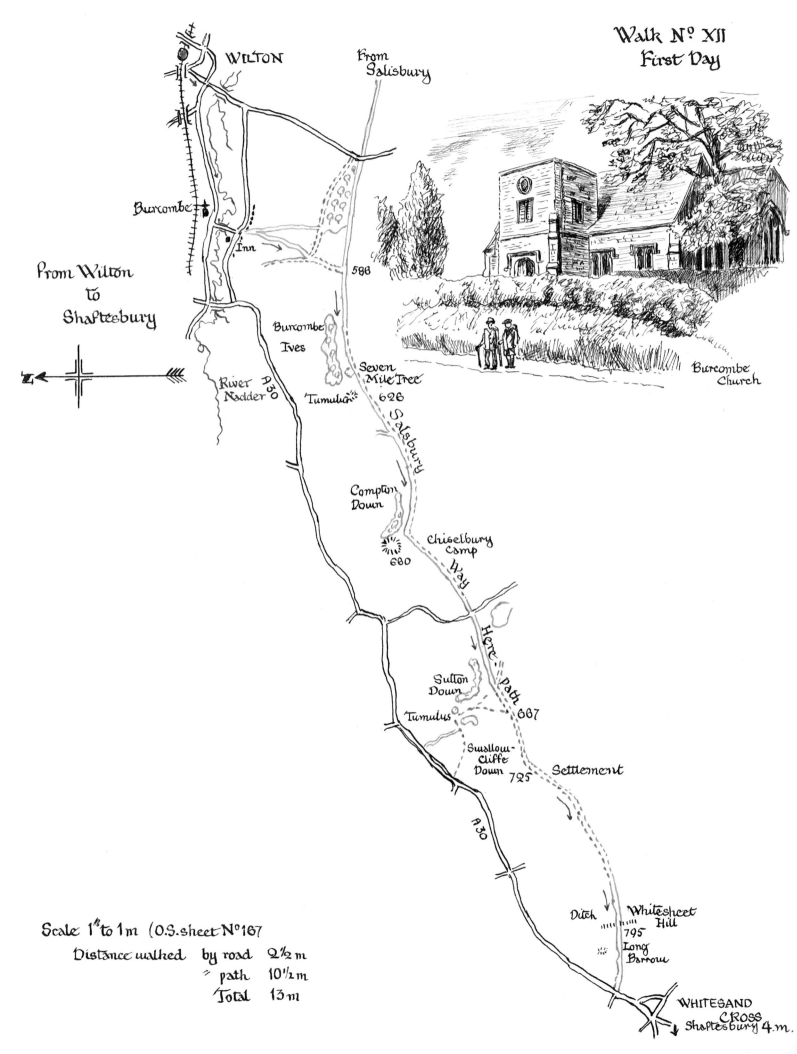

WILTON

From Salisbury

Walk Nº XII
First Day

Burcombe

Inn

From Wilton
to
Shaftesbury

N

586

Burcombe
Ives

River
Nadder

A 30

Seven
Mile Tree
626

Tumulus

Salisbury

Compton
Down

Chiselbury
Camp

680

Way

Here-
path

Sutton
Down

667

Tumulus

Swallow-
Cliffe
Down   725

Settlement

A 30

Burcombe
Church

Ditch

Whitesheet
Hill
795

Long
Barrow

Scale 1" to 1 m (O.S.sheet Nº 167

Distance walked   by road   2½ m
                  " path   10½ m
          Total   13 m

WHITESAND
CROSS
Shaftesbury 4 m

From Wilton to Shaftesbury *Monday 19th March 1962*

e set out on a cold and sunny day along the Nadder Valley from Wilton whither we had come by train. At Burcombe the church was pleasantly placed on a mound by the road but all that remains of interest was some long and short work in the outer wall of the chancel. A sign nearby directed us over the river to the Ship Inn. This was welcome for the long afternoon would find us on the open downs with no more inns till evening. South of the village lay a deep combe and at the head of it was Lyon's Barrow (printed on the map, presumably in error, as "borrow"). Near here we turned along the old ridge track known as "Salsbury Way". This trackway is one of the best preserved in all Wiltshire probably because it is high, dry, level and the shortest route from Salisbury to Shaftesbury. When it was in use as a coaching road in the 18th century, prominent trees took the place of milestones. Bernard Berry believed he had identified a number of these as lime trees. We noticed a lime in a beech grove above Burcombe Ivers; measured from Salisbury this could have been "Seven Mile Tree". We also wondered about the name "Herepath" given to this track and to the track from Marlborough Downs to Avebury. We now learn it is a Saxon word meaning a "Soldier's Path".

As we walked pursued by the wind we enjoyed wide views across the Nadder valley on our right and the Ebble on the left. Parallel to us on the south of the Ebble was a high ridge marking the course of the Ox Drove. Inevitably we planned to walk that trackway one day. At Chiselbury Camp we rested in the ditch facing the sun. Further west was evidence of ancient settlements near the long spur of Sutton Down. The silence along this ridge was broken only by the sound of a light plane which actually landed near us. We reached the highest point on Whitesheet Hill and then came down quickly past a chalk pit to the main road after four hours and ten miles of superb uninterrupted downland walking.

There was a milestone near Whitesand Cross inscribed "Shaston 4" which was Hardy's name for Shaftesbury. There was also a bus and as it was getting late and dark we took it gratefully. We put up at the "Crown" in Shaftesbury but had to look elsewhere for a meal. Both fish shops were closed and we were on the point of putting down half-a-guinea each for dinner when two small boys took us down the steep cobbles of Gold Hill to a secret place, which we could never find again, called St James Fish Bar. Here in an unkempt room we had the finest fish and chip supper ever which was only right and proper for was not James a fisherman?

From Shaftesbury
to
Stourton

N

Long Lane
Tumuli Whitesheet Hill
Stourhead
Hill Fort The
Stourton ✕ 802 Ditch Harrow Way
Zeals Knoll 604 Great Bottom
Long Hill Well Head
MERE

A 350
Great Ridgeway
A 303

The Lane

East Knoyle
Inn
Lower Leigh Fm

Shaftesbury Lane

Semley

Castle Rings
729
River Nadder
Wincombe Park
A 303

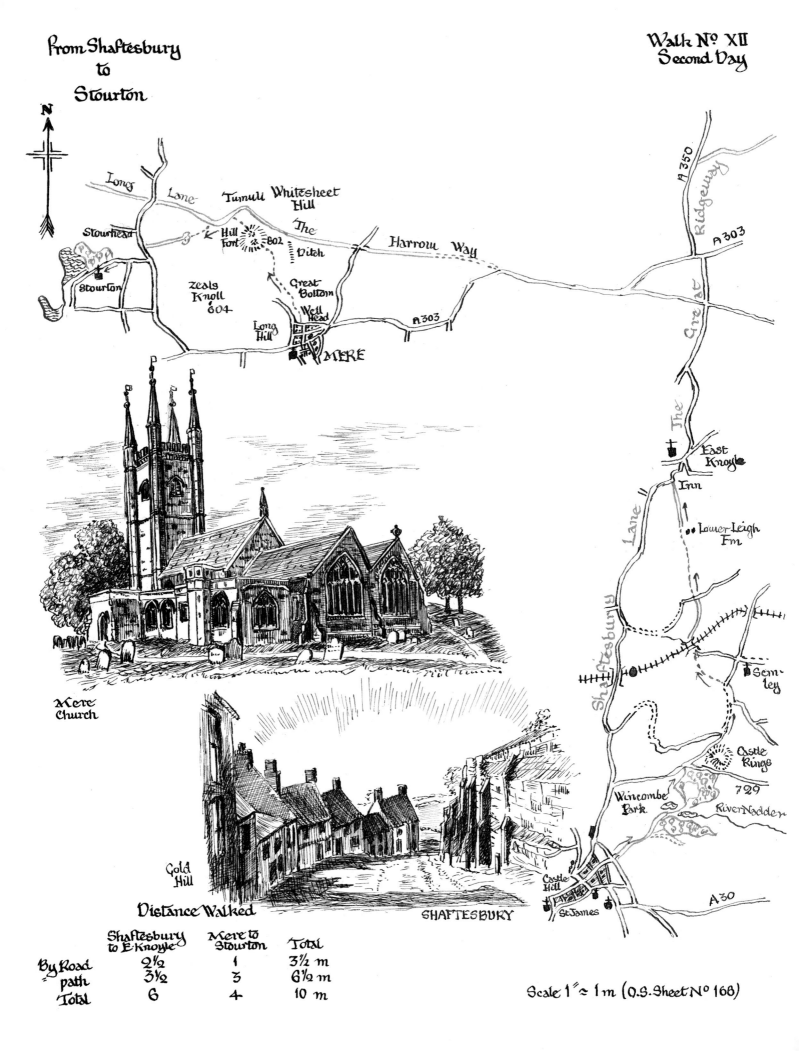

Mere Church

Gold Hill

SHAFTESBURY

Castle Hill
St James
A 30

Distance Walked

	Shaftesbury to E·Knoyle	Mere to Stourton	Total
By Road	2½	1	3½ m
path	3½	3	6½ m
Total	6	4	10 m

Scale 1″ ≃ 1 m (O.S. Sheet Nº 168)

From Shaftesbury to Stourton   *Tuesday 20th March*

All traffic was excluded from Shaftesbury because of work on a new sewer, so we had a quiet night at the Crown. Next morning we saw from the abbey ruins in this hilltop town a fine view to the south; northwards the countryside was shrouded in mist. The Great Ridgeway goes north from Shaftesbury by Shaftesbury Lane. As it is also the A350 we avoided it and were rewarded by the beauty of the lake in Wincombe Park. At Castle Rings, a huge earthworks, we rested in the ditch. "Get a load of this quiet!" said John from among the trees. If not elegant it was an eloquent remark and we fell silent also. From Tittlepath Hill we saw across the vale the outlines of Salisbury Plain and made our way towards them by a green lane that might have been the old road between Semley and East Knoyle. The mild and sunny weather encouraged us to saunter. The sight of labourers sitting on bales and sacks at Lower Leigh Farm nearly induced us to join them. The sun was bright enough to photograph our shadows on the road but there was no brilliant colour in the scene – only delicate pastel shades of grey and green and blue behind the dark tracery of bare trees.

In the Seymour Arms at East Knoyle the landlady asked us where we had escaped from – but she served us. We were afterwards conducted around the church by the verger and learned that the rectory was the home of Sir Christopher Wren. We had to reach Stourton by nightfall and because of our dilatory morning's walk we knew we could not visit both Mere church and Whitesheet Hill unless we took a bus – and the bus shelter at East Knoyle was a splendid suntrap! Suddenly therefore we were in Mere spending the time saved on the bus in the church of St Michael. It was a good church with a fine rood screen and a parvise over each porch. John was much interested in the rare Dominical letter 'E' on the brass of Sir John Bettesthorne of the late 14th century.

After a cup of tea we took a path to the foot of a spur from Whitesheet Hill. In the gathering dusk we rose quickly above the deep combe called Great Bottom, saw the shadowy odd shaped outlines of Long Hill and Zeal's Knoll and discerned some excellent examples of lynchetts hereabouts. We seemed to be among mountains climbing some band in the Lake District. The summit of Whitesheet Hill crowned by a hill fort loomed ahead. We went down it on the other side by the Harrow Way which goes on westwards as Long Lane (so called because it came from afar). Beyond a knoll south of Long Lane we found a green lane about thirty feet wide. This was something of a mystery for it began at the knoll and ended half a mile away at Stourton. In fact the entire route in semi-darkness from Mere to the floodlit Bristol cross in Stourton village was full of mystery and beauty.

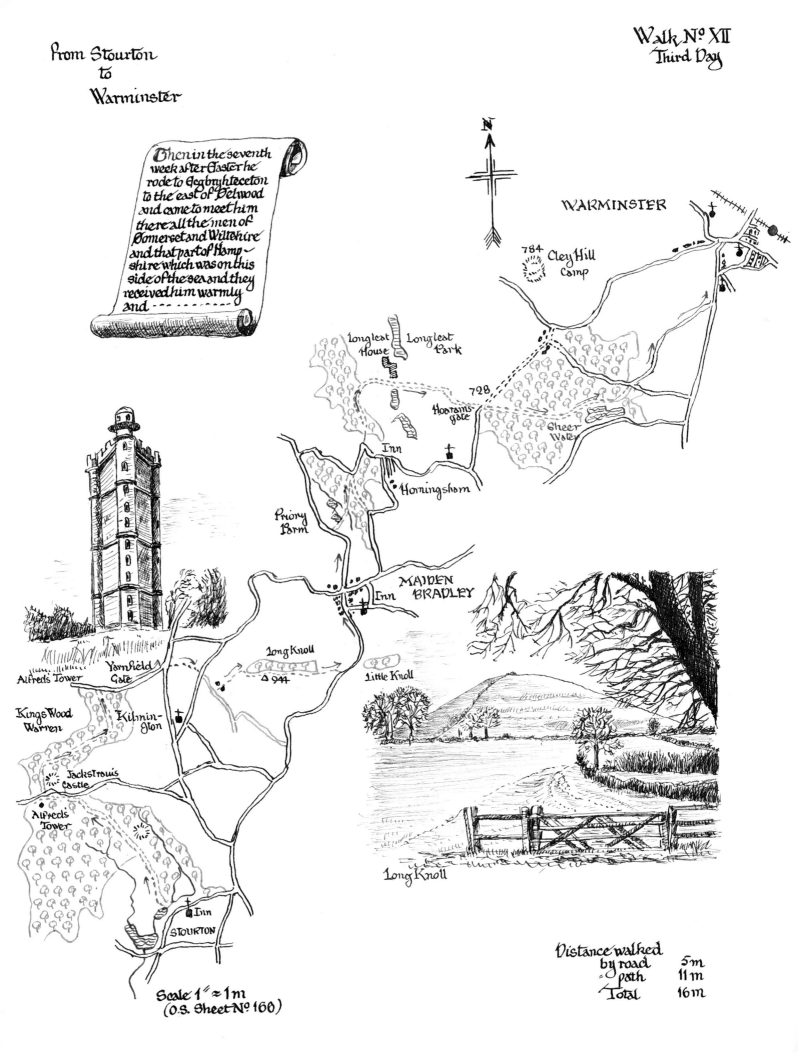

from Stourton
to
Warminster

Then in the seventh
week after Easter he
rode to Egbryhteceton
to the east of Selwood
and came to meet him
there all the men of
Somerset and Wiltshire
and that part of Hamp-
shire which was on this
side of the sea and they
received him warmly
and ----

N

WARMINSTER

784 Cley Hill
Camp

Longleat
House   Longleat
Park

728
Hoorainsgate

Sheer
Water

Inn

Horningsham

Priory
Farm

MAIDEN
BRADLEY

Inn

Long Knoll
△ 944

Little Knoll

Yarnfield
Gate

Alfreds Tower

Kings Wood
Warren

Kilmington

Jackstrouis
Castle

Alfred's
Tower

Long Knoll

Inn

STOURTON

Scale 1″ ≈ 1m
(O.S. Sheet No. 160)

Distance walked
by road   5m
by path   11m
Total   16m

From Stourton to Warminster   *Wednesday 21st March*

hen we left the Spreadeagle Inn the first live thing we saw was a peacock on the lawn. Here by Stourhead Gardens we were in 18th-century England. We passed by a stone arch and classical temples bordering the lake and climbed gently by a most pleasant path to the top of Kingsettle Hill and Alfred's Tower which is high enough to top a thousand feet above sea-level. This place on the borderland between the high downs of Wiltshire and the softer Somerset country was the turning point of our walk. It was so for Alfred who is said to have gathered his forces here before marching on to defeat the Danes at Edington in 879. As the line of march, the site of the battle and the final pursuit roughly corresponded with our route in these last three days, the passages in the Anglo-Saxon Chronicle describing these events are inset in the maps. We crossed the Harrow Way to the earthwork called Jack Straws Castle. Below here was a superb two-mile long terrace called Hanging Road looking out over Somerset with views to the Mendips. At Yarnfield Gate we took our first "non-path" to leave the wooded escarpment for Long Knoll, the highest hill in Wiltshire. It was scattered over with lumps of white chalk as though Alfred had done battle here only yesterday.

e came into Maiden Bradley with no food, to find the village store closed. However, the landlord of the Somerset Arms put up for us plates of meat, bread, cheese and onions. Lunching with us here was a chauffeur of rosy visage troubled neither by physical toil nor mental strife. Maiden Bradley lies on the watershed between the Wylye and the Frome which may account for the local legend of a stream running uphill. At Priory Farm we saw what little remained of the 12th-century hospital for leper maidens – now perpetuated in the name of the village. There was a leper-bowl in the wall like a holy-water stoup with a chute for pennies.

ince leaving King Alfred's Tower we had kept fairly closely to the so-called West Wilts trackway which links Harrow Way with the Cotswolds. Now the magnet of Longleat House drew us off course but proved disappointing. The house was closed, there were large parking signs before it and all the roads in the park were of asphalt. The Marquis of Bath spotting unappreciative aliens in his park picked us up in his land-rover and dropped us at the nearest exit which was called Heaven's Gate. Here was a long green lawn planted with shapely evergreens. Then we passed through deep woods to Shearwater where we saw the sun set over the lake through an oriel window. Then followed a long smooth descent to Warminster where we enjoyed soup and curry in a small cafe and were lucky to find in the King's Arms a room for the three of us at only twelve and sixpence each.

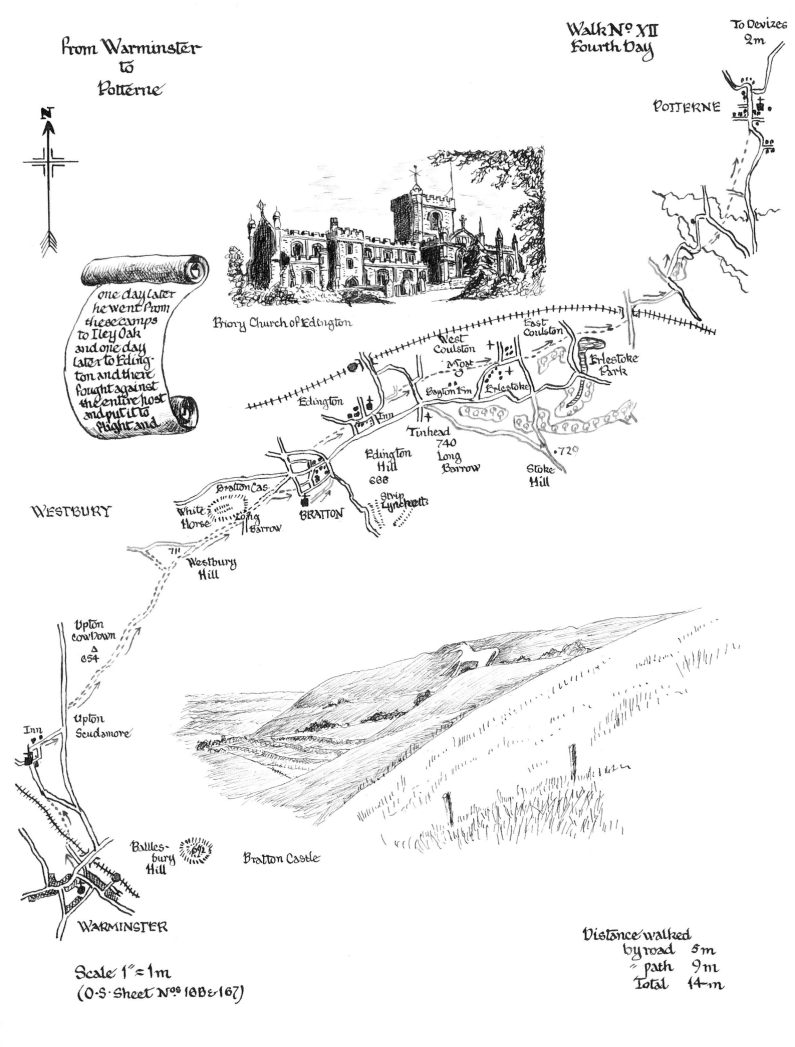

from Warminster
to
Potterne

N

To Devizes
2m

POTTERNE

one day later
he went from
these camps
to Iley Oak
and one day
later to Eding-
ton and there
fought against
the entire host
and put it to
flight and

Priory Church of Edington

West
Coulston

East
Coulston

Moat

Erlestoke
Park

Edington

Inn

Bayton Frm

Erlestoke

Tinhead
740
Long
Barrow

•729

Edington
Hill
688

Stoke
Hill

Bratton Cas.

Strip
Lynchett

WESTBURY

White
Horse

Long
Barrow

BRATTON

711

Westbury
Hill

Upton
Cowdown
△
654

Upton
Scudamore

Inn

Battles-
bury
Hill

Bratton Castle

WARMINSTER

Scale 1" = 1m
(O·S· Sheet Nºs 18B & 167)

Distance walked
by road   5m
" path   9m
Total   14·m

From Warminster to Devizes   *Thursday 22nd March*

In view of the long day ahead of us we made an early start across the meadows to Upton Scudamore where in the church we saw the mutilated effigies of the Scudamore family and pre-fabricated arcade, still unopened, in the south wall. Soon we were climbing a spur of the downs between the escarpment and a firing range. There was also a deep chalk pit and a crushing plant but the downs resumed their ageless aspect when we came in sight of the Westbury White Horse said to commemorate Alfred's great victory over the Danes. Older still was the Iron Age earthworks called Bratton Castle from whose huge ramparts we looked down to the Vale – a setting akin to the Vale of White Horse viewed from Uffington Castle. Approaching Bratton church in the combe below by a causeway of steps in a deep wooded ravine we saw a badger. Once he stopped and half turned so that we clearly saw the white stripes on his head. Beyond Bratton, whose church in Transitional Perpendicular style was a gem, we followed paths by a stream behind the village and came to the Plough at Edington. Having a tiny parlour with a large open fire and no bar it seemed more like a private than a public house.

The Priory Church of Edington was part of an Augustinian monastery of Bonshommes – one of only two such settlements in the country. In the south transept was a stone effigy of one of the canons under a painted canopy. It bore a rebus of a barrel or tun with a sprig in it. This is attributed to John Beckington or Baynton depending on whether the sprig is of beech or bay. In support of both theories there is a Beckington near Westbury and Baynton Farm near Edington. The church was magnificent and showed like Bratton, but on a grander scale, the transition from Decorated to Perpendicular style. It would be dark in three hours and Potterne, our next objective, was eight miles distant so we took the most direct route through Pewsey Vale resting but once among alders and bulrushes by a lake in Erlestoke Park. We glimpsed a kingfisher along a stream and were asked by an old man if a war had started. Then on a long field path an ancient hairy swain with two gawping girls looked at us in astonishment saying "No one ever walked this path these days."

At half past six we put on the lights in Potterne church and the Rev Davies came to see who we were. He had been visited recently by John Betjeman. He enthused for an hour about the Saxon font (inscribed in runes, "like as the hart desireth the water brooks"), the dole stone, the old north door, repairs to the roof and other matters. But Potterne was indeed a church to enthuse over. It was like Salisbury cathedral in miniature, cruciform and with plain lancets and shafts of Purbeck. We got a drink and a bus, found the White Lion in Devizes and were content. We had been out for over twelve hours.

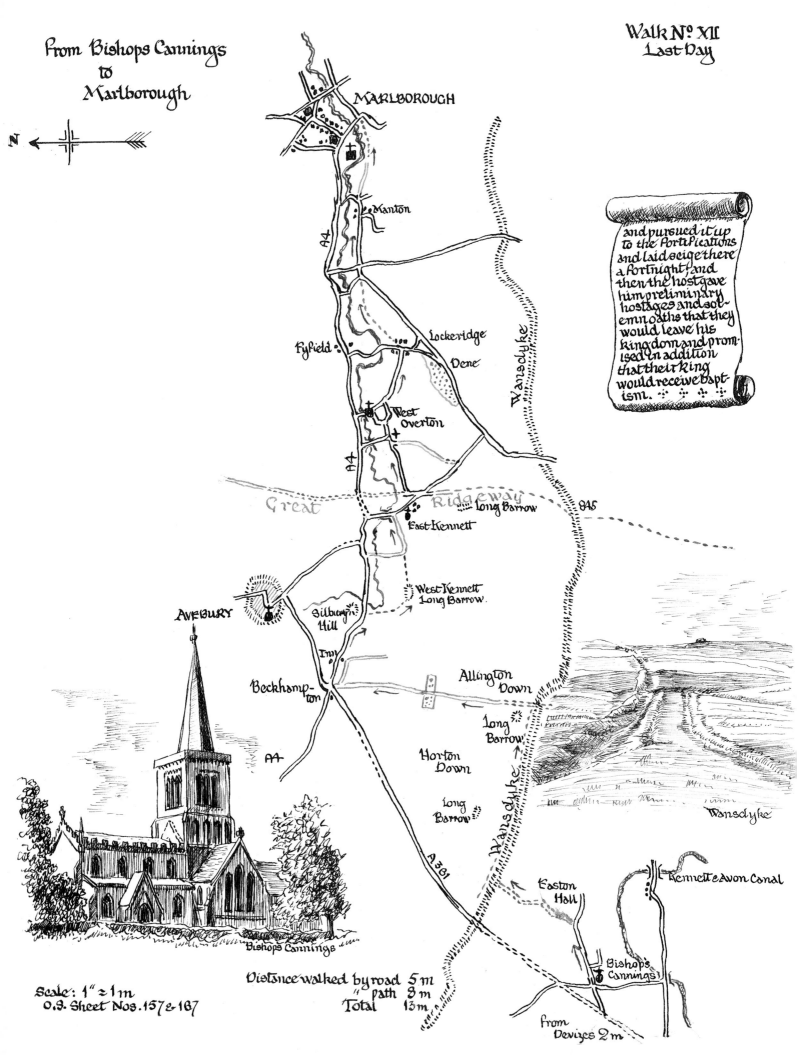

From Bishops Cannings
to
Marlborough

N

MARLBOROUGH

Manton

A4

Fyfield

Lockeridge
Dene

Wansdyke

West
Overton

A4

Great   Ridgeway   845

Long Barrow

East Kennett

West Kennett
Long Barrow.

AVEBURY

Silbury
Hill

Inn

Beckhamp-
ton

Allington Down

Long
Barrow

A4

Horton
Down

Long
Barrow

Wansdyke

Wansdyke

A361

Easton
Hall

Kennett & Avon Canal

Bishops Cannings

Bishop's
Cannings

from
Devizes 2 m

Scale: 1" ≈ 1 m
O.S. Sheet Nos. 157 & 187

Distance walked by road 5 m
            "   path 8 m
Total   13 m

and pursued it up
to the fortifications
and laid seige there
a fortnight, and
then the host gave
him preliminary
hostages and sol-
emn oaths that they
would leave his
kingdom and prom-
ised in addition
that their king
would receive bapt-
ism.

From Devizes to Marlborough   *Friday 23rd March*

evizes means "ad divisas" – at the divisions between the hundreds of Potterne and Cannings. But it also stands at the division or watershed between the Wiltshire Avon and Somerset Avon. There is a road along this watershed from Salisbury Plain to Marlborough Downs called "Lydeway" but the Great Ridgeway crosses the Vale of Pewsey further east. By crossing the fields to Potterne yesterday we had cut a corner and missed both trackways. On this final morning we visited the church of St John with its low vaulted Norman chancel and a 14th-century street called St John's Alley. But the church of St Mary was locked and so was the museum. So we took leave of Devizes on a 'bus and began our walk proper at Bishops Cannings. Here was a most lovely grey stone church, cruciform with Norman arcading and Early English triple lancets. An unusual piece of furniture was the Meditation pew on which was painted a large hand bearing dismal moral maxims in Latin.

nd then we climbed the scarp of the Marlborough Downs in the teeth of a gale. The great plateau looked grim under a black north sky which would soon bring snow. Across our path near the top of the Downs we came upon the long earthwork called Wansdyke which extends east and west for some sixty miles and is probably fifteen hundred years old. We followed it for some distance marvelling at the depth of the ditch and the steepness of the bank. Nobody seems to know why it was constructed. We turned north into the broad familiar valley of the upper Kennett littered with sarsens and tumuli and, faintly discernible in the distance, the great mound of Silbury. Escaping for a time from the wind and snow in the Wagon and Horses at Beckhampton we learned to our dismay that Marlborough station was closed and we would have to find another way home. In the meantime we visited the West Kennett Long Barrow which was fully opened and naturally lit via a pane of glass let into the turf. There were in it five chambers separated by huge stones and at the door was a stone which, according to John, was intended to stop motorists driving in. Aiming now to catch a bus from Marlboro' to Swindon we had a forced march of some six miles through the Kennett villages seeing about as little of them as we would have done from a car and not stopping either for a church or a rest. We missed the famous sarsens at Lockeridge Dene and were assisted by the white-painted stiles on a waymarked footpath. But we succeeded in missing the bus. We say "succeeded" for this enabled us to enjoy to the full an enormous pot of tea (giving each of us eleven cups) in a small cafe, to look at our "pieds poudrés" and count our good fortune in having dry, if dusty going on this our first long spring walk.

The End of the Twelfth Walk

John Chapman, tinker, dreamed a dreame
In Swaffham town so fair
To hie him he to London Bridge
And meet a stranger there,
Who'd fill his days with happiness
He'd never know more care.

He took his staff ~ he took his bag
He wended on his way,
The neighbours laughed, they bowted him
They tried to say him nay
But he indeed ne'er heeded them
Nor what they had to say.

An old man met him on the Bridge
To whom his tale he told.
The stranger laughed and said "I dream'd
About a pile of gold
On a tinker's land in Swaffham town;
'Tis foolish I do hold".

Without a word the tinker turned
To retrace every mile,
And took his spade and dug his land
To find his golden pile
And in thanksgiving he did build
A steeple and an aisle.

Walsyngham

Bitter, bitter, oh to behould
    the grasse to growe
Where the walles of Walsingham
    so statly did shewe. ❖

Such were the workes of Walsingham
    while shee did stande
Such are the wrackes as now do shewe
    of that holy land! ❖

Levell, levell with the ground
    the towres do lye,
Which with their golden glittering tops
    pearsed once to the skye. ❖

There weare gates, no gates are nowe;
    the waies unknown
Where the presse of pearses did passe
    while her fame far was blowen ❖

Oules do scrike wher the sweetest himnes
    lately weer sunge;
Toades and serpentes hold their dennes
    where the Palmers did thronge. ❖

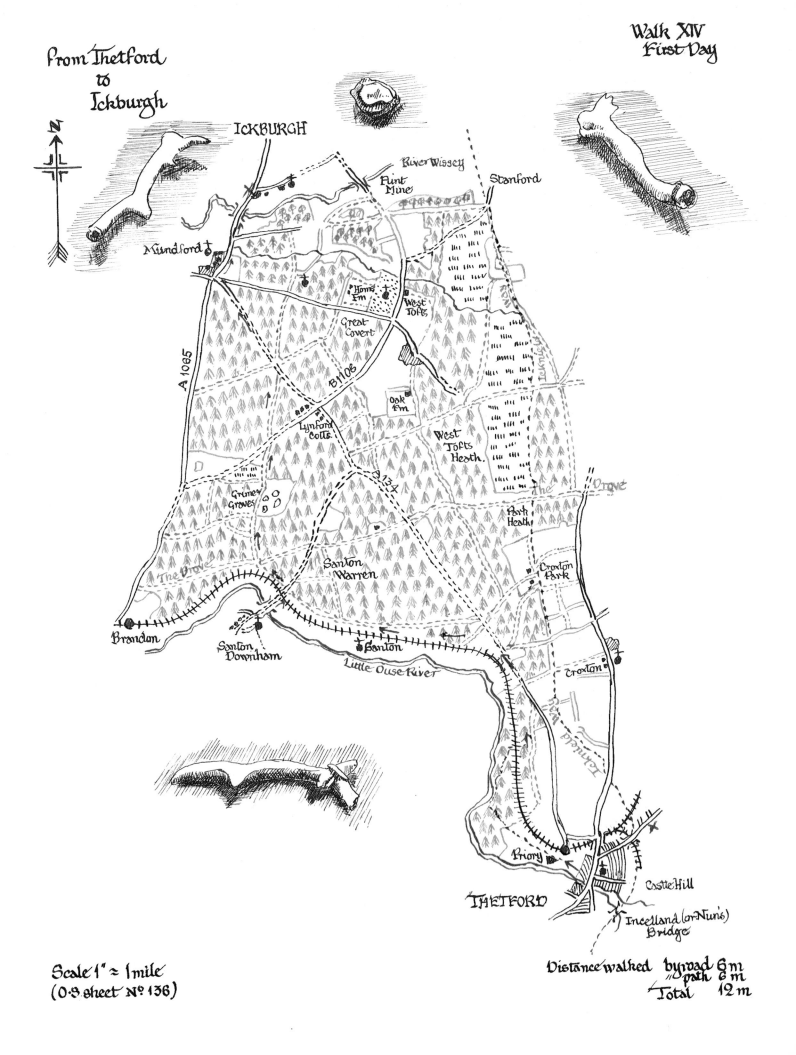

From Thetford
to
Ickburgh

N

Walk XIV
First Day

ICKBURGH

River Wissey

Flint Mine

Stanford

Mundford

Home Fm

West Tofts

Great Covert

B1108

A 1065

Oak Fm

Lynford Cotts

West Tofts Heath

The Drove

Grimes Groves

A 134

Park Heath

The Drove

Croxton Park

Santon Warren

Brandon

Santon Downham

Santon

Little Ouse River

Railway Line

Croxton

Priory

THETFORD

Castle Hill

Incelland (or Nun's) Bridge

Scale 1" ≈ 1 mile
(O.S. sheet Nº 136)

Distance walked by road 6 m
path 6 m
Total 12 m

The Norfolk Walk

Breckland

Monday 11th March 1963

ick had suggested a tour in Norfolk to include the Icknield Way, the great medieval shrine to Our Lady at Walsingham and the Neolithic flint mines known as Grimes Graves. We took a train to Thetford on the Sunday evening and stayed in a private bungalow near the Ark Inn – our first call. In the morning our first call was to the ruin of St Mary's Priory, a former Cluniac House and once one of the greatest monastic houses in East Anglia. Apart from the gatehouse only rough, flinty foundations remained. Thetford lies in the heart of a barren, sandy region called "Breckland", as alien to Norfolk as Dartmoor is to Devon. The flinty untilled areas or "brecks" are unfenced and probably appear as they did in prehistoric times. There are huge plantations of conifers in military array – and there is the army. Pat had written to the War Department Estate Office to find out if we could walk from Thetford to Swaffham northward via the Icknield Way. He was told that our proposed route was closed to the public in the Stanford training area, that we could visit Grimes Graves but would thence have to follow the Queen's Highway (sic) for the most part.

e left the Priory in steady rain to cross the brecks. Only a little group of double snowdrops relieved the general gloom which deepened when plastic trousers and a gascape were torn crossing barbed wire. We came by Santon and its rebuilt flint church to Santon Downham just over the Little Ouse river into Suffolk. This is a large village and headquarters of the Breckland foresters – but there was no inn. We took shelter and lunch in the church porch the very stones of which dripped moisture inside as the frost thawed out. Not far away in a wide breck surrounded by woods were the shallow pits called Grimes Graves long before Canon Greenwell discovered what they were in 1870. Two pits had been excavated thirty feet down through the top layers of sand and boulder clay to the flint strata beneath. One pit was roofed over with glass like the West Kennet Long Barrow. We descended by iron ladders and saw at the bottom the openings into the galleries and a pile of flints and red deer antler picks. In the Ministry of Works hut were flint hammers, scrapers and even miners' lamps made from hollowed out lumps of chalk. There are signs of at least three hundred pits in the area showing that the industry was most extensive. The rest of our journey northward was uneventful and less wet. The walk ended at Ickburgh in a cafe on the Queen's Highway. As it was late we persuaded a van driver to take us to Swaffham. Here in the White Lion the landlord's daughter, hearing of our urge to go out walking every March and October remarked, "You mean you feel like migrating birds?"

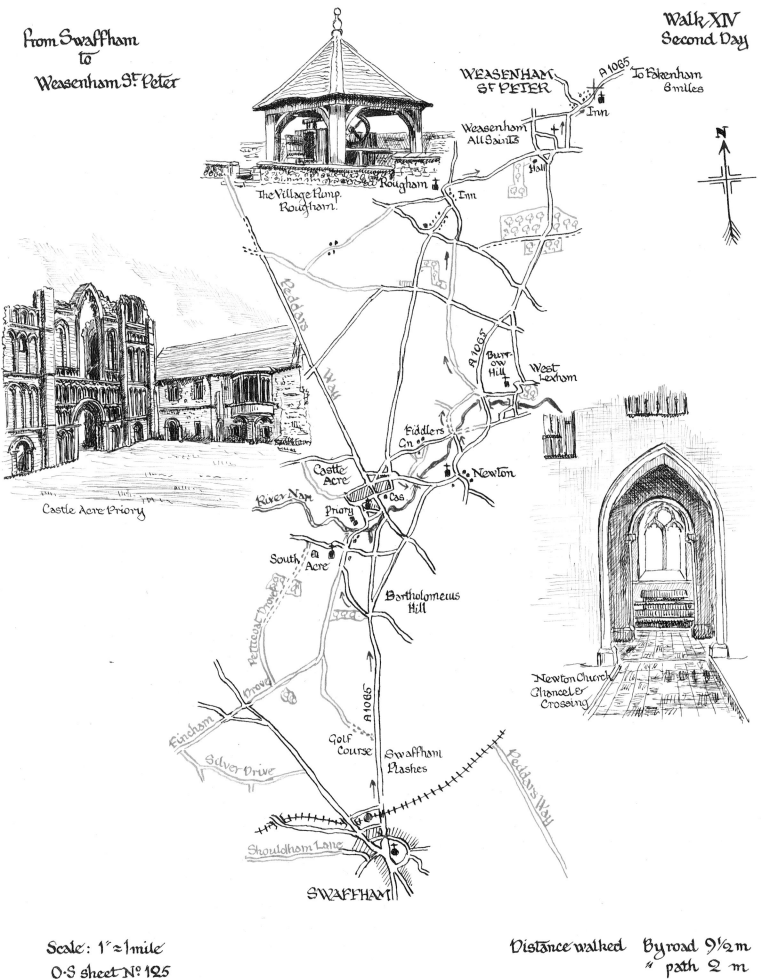

From Swaffham
to
Weasenham St. Peter

Walk XIV
Second Day

The Village Pump.
Rougham.

Castle Acre Priory

Newton Church
Chancel &
Crossing

WEASENHAM
ST PETER

A 1065   To Fakenham
6 miles

Inn

Weasenham
All Saints

Hall

Rougham

Inn

A 1065

Burr-
ow
Hill

West
Lexham

Fiddlers
Cn

Newton

Castle
Acre

River Nar

Priory   Cas.

South
Acre

Bartholomeus
Hill

Petticoat Drove

Fincham Drove

Silver Drive

A 1065

Golf
Course

Swaffham
Plashes

Peddars Way

Peddars Way

Shouldham Lane

SWAFFHAM

N

Scale: 1″ ≈ 1 mile
O·S sheet Nº 125
Start and finish at X

Distance walked   By road 9½ m
               „ path 2 m
       Total   11½ m

Acreland   *Tuesday 12th March 1963*

Knitting quietly in the parlour at the White Lion was Miss Granville-Smith, daughter of a former vicar. She was over ninety and in good health. She related the ancient ballad about the Swaffham Pedlar retold in fewer verses on an earlier page. In the church we met Mr Fred Knock; he was over eighty and in his fifty-third year as verger. He pointed out the carvings of the pedlar and his wife and showed us the famous 15th-century Black Book of Accounts which mentions the pedlar as a church benefactor. Then he brought out the most precious possession of this church, a Book of Hours of about 1420. John studied the lavish illumination for some time, stored it away in his mind and, weeks later, reproduced this style in the preface to the spring walk of 1955. We were thus far behind with our records.

The map showed a number of named green droves to the north including the Peddars Way, but as time was short and the distance shorter we took the road for the "Acres". Skies were grey as we went north past fields of frosted kale now rotting in the warmer weather. Patches of snow still remained from the great frost of last month. The country was generally bare but the church of South Acre was almost hidden by trees. It was fairly small and contained a few brasses. Close by the River Nar was the ruined Cluniac priory founded in the 11th century. It was the most complete monastic remain we had yet seen. The west front of this priory church was very imposing and the Norman porch and Prior's Lodging were still intact. We visited the spacious church in Castleacre containing fine woodwork in pulpit, font cover and screen. We also visited the "Albert Victor" inn and walked about the little flint town. It lies within the outer bailey of the castle and appears unchanged since the Middle Ages. A castle gateway stands across the top of Bailey Street which looks like Gold Hill in Shaftesbury. We saw yet another church at Newton near Castleacre. It was small and narrow with chancel, nave and central Norman tower, the transepts having fallen. It was plain and unrestored and refreshing.

We crossed the little River Nar a third time and followed it upstream through rough reedy meadows and among little hills that had a look of Ireland. We approached Rougham by a wide green lane that was shown as metalled on our map; maybe it had reverted through disuse. At the Crown Inn they made tea for us while we visited the church. We had tried no inn for tea outside opening hours since we were refused at East Meon five years before. While tractors with headlamps were ploughing in the dark we walked steadily on the road for about an hour until the Fakenham bus overtook us at Weasenham St Peter. Later we found a fish and chips bar in Fakenham and settled down in the Windsor bar of the Red Lion to plan the morrow's route.

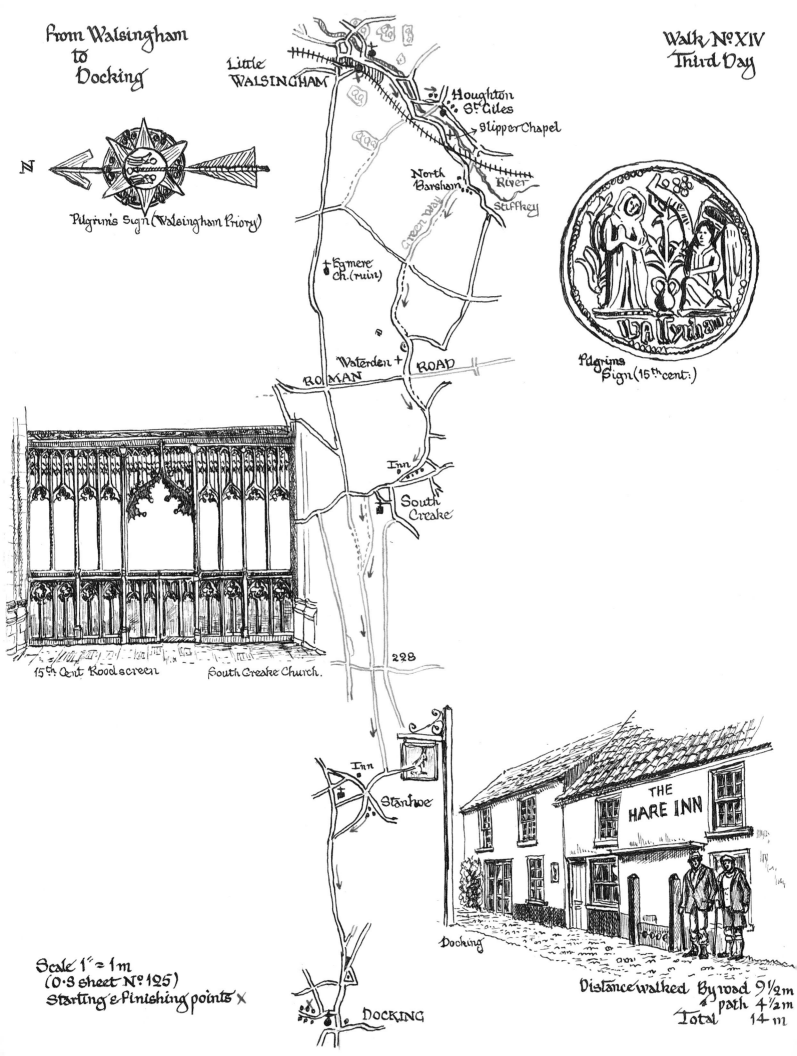

from Walsingham
to
Docking

Little
WALSINGHAM

Walk Nº XIV
Third Day

N

Pilgrim's Sign (Walsingham Priory)

Houghton
St Giles

Slipper Chapel

North
Barsham

River
Stiffkey

Green Way

† Egmere
Ch. (ruin)

Waterden † ROAD

ROMAN

Inn

South
Creake

228

Pilgrims
Sign (15th cent.)

15th Cent Rood screen   South Creake Church.

Inn

Stanhoe

THE
HARE INN

Docking

Scale 1″ = 1 m
(O·S sheet Nº 125)
Starting & Finishing points X

DOCKING

Distance walked By road 9½ m
path 4½ m
Total 14 m

Holyland   *Wednesday 13th March 1963*

ny road to the Holy Shrine was called a Walsingham Way. The Way from London passed through Thetford and Fakenham. We latter-day pilgrims took train from Fakenham to save time. It was a perfect morning. We lingered in the empty but sun-filled streets, bought wholemeal bread from an ancient bakery and called at the Anglican shrine, claimed to be on the site of the former Holy House. The Augustinian priory nearby was also said to have housed the shrine. From what little remained John visualised the ground-plan and Mick recognised in some vaulting a style like that of Michelham priory. We went on to the parish church to find to our dismay that it had nearly been destroyed by fire. The famous Seven Sacrament font was apparently unharmed but was boarded up. We saw the ruins of the Franciscan friary founded in 1348 to minister to the needs of pilgrims. In 1937 the Franciscans returned to Greyfriars in Walsingham where they have a chapel and hostels for modern pilgrims. A mile down the road towards Fakenham were two former pilgrim chapels. That at Houghton St Giles was on the Walsingham Way from London and has a rich screen with painted panels. The other on the pilgrims' road from Lynn is the so-called Slipper Chapel – a beautiful 14th-century building restored to Catholic use in recent years and now the chief objective of Catholic pilgrims. Here the crowned statue of Our Lady was surrounded by a blaze of candles and flowers. But such modern devotion could not conceal the "wrackes of that holy lande" described in the Elizabethan ballad which we have written down in these pages.

fter nearly three hours around Walsingham we walked west over a wide deserted upland by ancient half-metalled pilgrim roads. The churches were in decay: the shell of Egmere stood to the north and Waterden, which we came to by a green strip in the ploughland, had dry rot in the floor, damp in the walls and an empty vicarage – a dead living. John and Mick marched fast and reached the Ostrich Inn half an hour before closing time; when Pat arrived only twenty minutes remained. John Betjeman ranked South Creake with Thaxted, Blisland and Horley (Oxon) among the perfect village churches. Certainly the memory of it remained long after we had left the cool space and light and whiteness beneath the painted angels in the hammerbeam roof. We set off again by a good track between sparse hedges and arable. Occasional bracken, broom and whin added colour to the scene. When the desire for tea came upon us we called at the Nelson Inn at Stanhoe and we were again successful. Much refreshed we finished the journey by road as darkness and rain were beginning to fall. Our destination was once known as "Dry Docking" but there were well-filled ponds in the fields. However, the Hare Inn was a welcome "dry dock". To our surprise and amusement it was kept by a Mr Leveret!

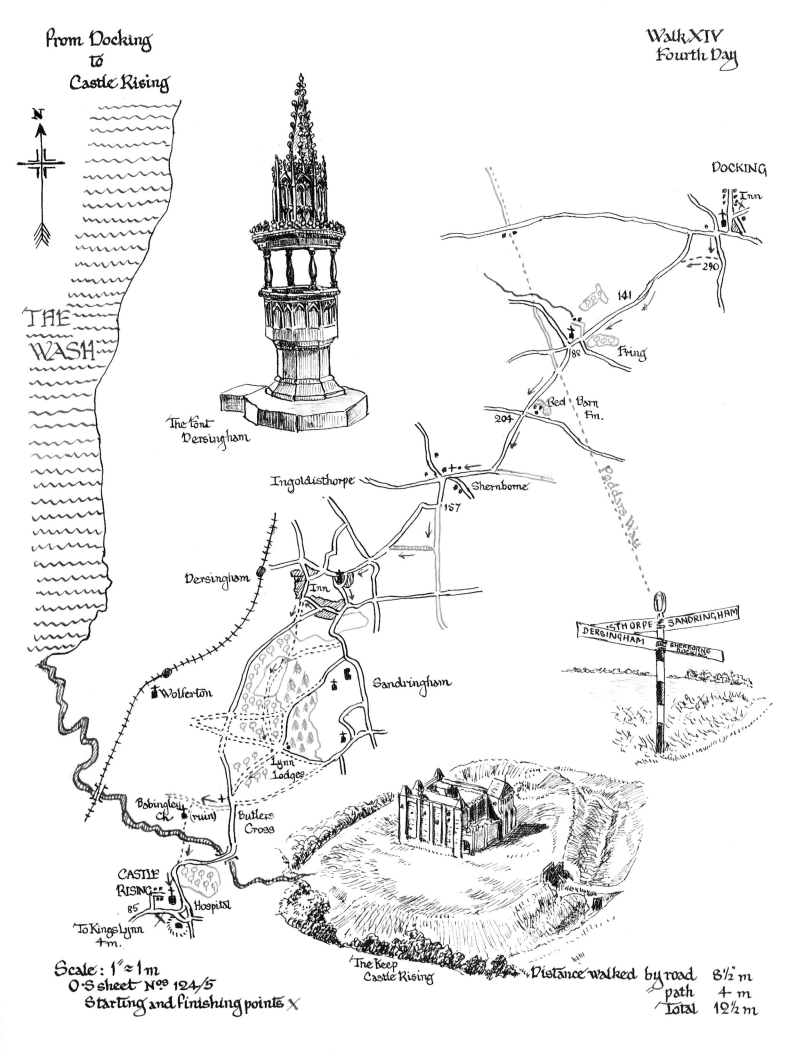

N

THE WASH

DOCKING

Inn

←290

141

Fring

88

Red Barn Fm.

204

Pedders Way

The Font Dersingham

Ingoldisthorpe

Shernborne

157

Dersingham

Inn

'STHORPE   SANDRINGHAM
DERSINGHAM   SHERBORNE
DOCKING

Wolferton

Sandringham

Lynn Lodges

Babingley Ch. (ruin)

Butlers Cross

CASTLE RISING

85

Hospital

To Kings Lynn 4 m.

The Keep Castle Rising

Scale: 1" ≈ 1 m
O·S sheet Nos 124/5
Starting and finishing points X

Distance walked by road   8½ m
          path   4 m
          Total   12½ m

Crown Land *Thursday 14th March 1963*

he Hare Inn at Docking was an ancient house. An apple rolled freely across the bedroom floor; but the beds were good, we didn't roll out and it cost us only 12/6d each. We went away past the waterworks and descended easily by a long lane to Fring where five lanes met. This was a charming place at the head of Heacham river. The church stood on a green knoll among a few big trees, and in it was a large wall painting of St Christopher. Soon we crossed the Peddars Way, a superb grass track, which we would have followed if it had gone in our direction. Beyond Red Barn Farm tractors coming off the fields had used the broad green verges to clean mud off the wheels. Pat, whose feet were sore, wished local authorities would allow all rural roads to revert to grass. After all, there were more tractors than cars in these parts.

he church at Shernborne was locked which was disappointing as we had hoped to see the font and a brass. Off the road to Dersingham Mick and John made a diversion and were rewarded by seeing a shepherd putting new-born lambs into sacks. Pat who stayed on the road was rewarded by thus reducing their lead over him. Dersingham church was of local carrstone and much restored but there were a few features of interest including a chest and a font. The village was neat and prosperous, no doubt because it was near Sandringham. We passed two hotels that were far too splendid for us and then found another "Albert Victor" where a friendly landlord recalled a longstanding rivalry between two of his customers – a coachman and a groom. He also explained why single bar pubs in Norfolk were so common: the "saloon bar people" went to the hotels. It was not a new democratic trend. At last after so many miles of road we found a glorious high level path in the Sandringham estate. From the very modest altitude of one hundred feet we looked between pines and rhododendrons across the marshes to the sea. In the marsh itself stood the ivy-clad ruin of Babingley church – the first Christian foundation of St Felix in East Anglia. At the turn of the century the Prince of Wales had built an unsightly ironclad thatched church at Butlers Cross, when he more happily could have rebuilt the ancient church nearby.

y ditches and plough we resumed the road at Castle Rising. There was just time to see the Norman keep of the castle before we boarded a bus for King's Lynn. If we had skimped Castle Rising by missing the church and old hospital we did less than justice to King's Lynn. St Margarets' deserved an hour to itself but at least we saw the two fine Flemish brasses, one of which was the "Braunche" or Peacock Feast brass of the late 14th-century. John scented the remains of a priory after observing some ancient lectern benches in the choir and then found the remainder of the monastic buildings embodied among nearby cottages adjacent to the Hanseatic warehouses. But we never found the pilgrim chapel of Our Lady of the Red Mount. Later in the evening we met Mr and Mrs Eggleton at a quiet pub in the close, arranged to meet Egg on the morrow and retired to the Rummer Hotel for the night.

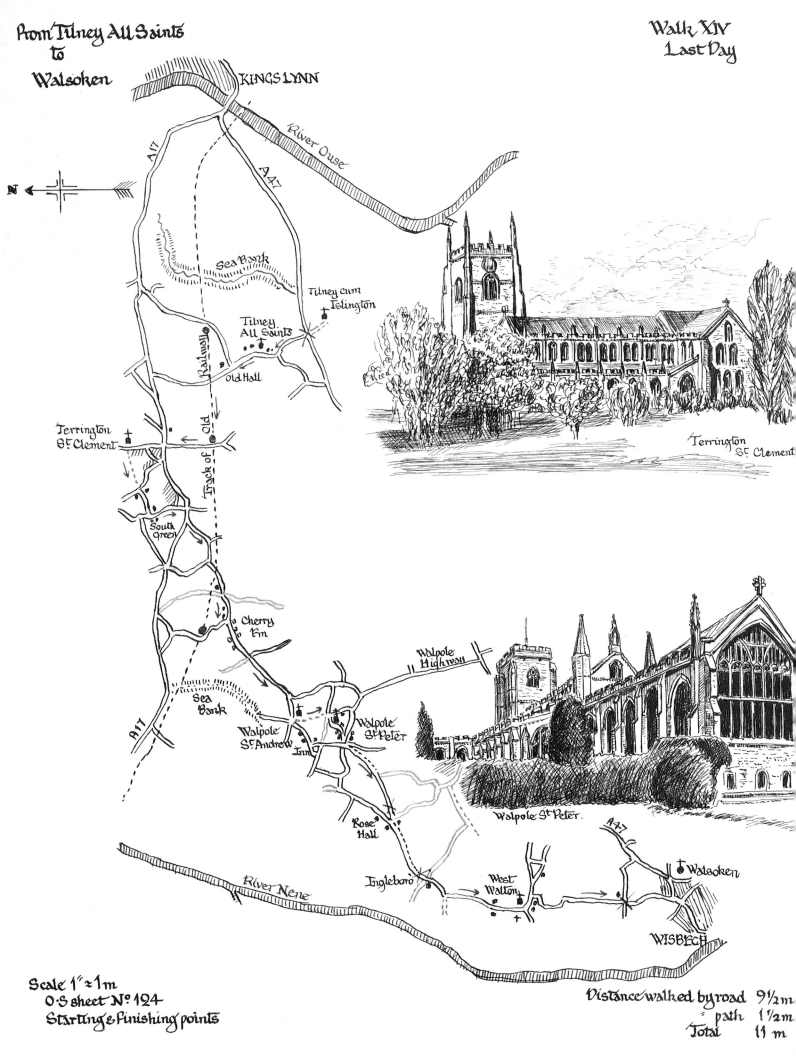

From Tilney All Saints
to
Walsoken

Walk XIV
Last Day

KINGS LYNN

River Ouse

A17

A47

Sea Bank

Railway

Tilney cum Islington

Tilney All Saints

Old Hall

Track of Old

Terrington St Clement

South Green

Cherry Fm

Walpole Highway

Sea Bank

A17

Walpole St Andrew

Inn

Walpole St Peter

Rose Hall

River Nene

Ingleboro'

West Walton

A47

Walsoken

WISBECH

Terrington St Clement

Walpole St Peter.

Scale 1" ≈ 1m
O.S sheet Nº 124
Starting & Finishing points

Distance walked by road   9½ m
                    path   1½ m
              Total   11 m

Marshland   *Friday 15th March 1963*

We left the Wisbech bus between the church towers of Tilney All Saints and Tilney cum Islington. Egg was waiting to accompany us. Farm workers opening up "tatey-graves" stopped work as we went up the lane to Tilney All Saints – a spacious church of Barnack stone with Norman arcades and a pine double hammerbeam roof. Cutting across the lanes by the disused track of an old railway we came to Terrington St Clement and its huge church, the "Cathedral of the Marshes". There were flying buttresses and high capped turrets and a separate tower that has served as a place of refuge when the sea broke through. Outside the village, planks were laid across the roadside ditches. In the past, said Egg, men would carry corn over these in four bushel sacks called coombs. He once knew a man who could thus carry a coomb weighing eighteen stones under each arm. A long way ahead were the church towers of the two Walpole villages while those of Terrington and Tilney could still be seen behind. The rich dark fields were ploughed to the ditches. Soon there appeared apple orchards and strawberry fields near Walpole St Andrew where the 15th-century church did not detain us for long. In the Plough Inn the locals discussed us among themselves. Eventually one came forward and said, "Do you mind telling us who you are and what you're doing?" When we told them and they knew Egg was a Walpole man they bought us a round of drinks.

The Walpoles are linked by the "Chase", an ancient paved path by which we came to the church of St Peter. It is claimed to be the most beautiful parish church in England. At a festival in June it would be decorated with flowers. Egg had close connexions with this church – the lychgate was built by his father-in-law and he was married there. We had declined an offer by one of the "Plough" men of a "lift" to the next two churches, but we accepted a short lift on a flat trailer drawn by a tractor. It took us close to Ingleborough where Egg would show us the mill with six sails. The mill had gone but in the farmhouse was a picture of it standing in a field of tulips. Now West Walton church and its separated tower appeared ahead. In all England there is no finer example of Early English work in a church; it was a veritable forest of Purbeck and even marbled detached shafts, but neither space now or time then would allow us to dwell on it. Egg's brother-in-law waited down the road to whisk us off to Walsoken, but the church was locked and we only glimpsed the rich Norman work through a crack in the door. Then followed tea with the Eggletons at Millfield in Walpole Highway presided over by Mrs Bunting and then a ride back to London in Egg's car.

The "Beatus" page contrasts pedlar and pilgrim. The pedlar had sought riches afar yet found them at home while the pilgrim had gone to make an act of penance or devotion. For each the way was hard whether Peddars Way or Walsingham Way. For us the entire journey was an end in itself and only hard when the road was made up.

The End of the Fourteenth Walk

MILESTONES: The Romans
used to hold a quinquennial census followed
by a sacrificial feast or "lustrum" which has
come to mean a five-year period. We have
counted the miles rather than the heads and
set them down for the first and second
lustra in an Itinerarium and Walkers
Wisdom at the end of each volume. Analogy with the famous cricket
statistics is but slight; rain never stopped play nor did we seek by furious
walking to break earlier records, rather did we go on walking at whim
until old records were broken by chance. In the same sort of way, temp-
erately, are weather records broken from time to time. Even so records
long unbeaten become as interesting as the newcomers which displace
them. Thus we find, on examining the personal mileages that Val walked 500 miles before he died and that John has never missed a walk nor a
mile of walking, a record never to be surpassed. The "County Championship"
which was held by Kent at the close of Volume I has passed to Sussex which
has a strong lead over all other counties. Belloc would have been pleased
to learn we had trod mostly his own favourite and most favoured county
west of Arun but he would not have known of another pertinent factor—
that here somewhere near Duncton lies the place equidistant from our
three homes though nearer to our hearts. We also notice that our average
daily mileage is falling, no doubt with advancing age. On the other hand
our annual mileage is rising perhaps because of decreasing family
commitments. We find that only once have we walked more than twenty
miles in a day and would not wish to exceed that figure again unless the
inns were so distant. Similarly, high mileages before lunch like the

memorable Ox Drove (Iter XVI) usually arise in an effort to reach an inn before closing time. The longest Iter of all remains the first from Winchester to Canterbury but too frequent recourse to "wheeled things" has prevented us from making a continuous walk longer than Iter II.

The incidence of footpaths is of particular interest in an age when the roads are cluttered with cars. Among intensively cultivated and industrialised countries of the world there is probably none which can offer such a wealth of footpaths as England. We have so far walked on about 500 miles of paths or track. In the first lustrum (1953~1958) nearly half our mileage was by paths but in the second it was well over half. We can scarcely hope for a better route in this particular time when we found sixteen miles of path in a day between Salisbury and Tollard Royal. The ideal would be a day entirely upon grass.

We may presume to look ahead just four years to the time of writing at the end of the third lustrum and record that in this volume, Dorset will challenge Sussex strongly for the County Championship while Hampshire and Kent will contend for third place ~ we cannot be certain until the mileages are calculated more accurately. Certainly the Icknield Way will prove longer by a few miles than the Pilgrims Way. Furthermore we will pass the thousandth milestone, the hundredth day and the twenty fifth Iter ~ miles of memories that will remain long after they are changed by Act of Parliament to Kilometres. We cannot set milestones by the way as the Romans did; we can only put them down in this book. They are all there in the Walkers Wisden and in the Itineraria whose format we owe to some unknown Roman who lived in the Reign of Antonine. 24th March· 1968

John · Caterham · Surrey · Pat · Bracknell · Berks · Mick · Seaford · Sussex

IMP · CÆS · SEPT · SEVERVS · A · VIN · DOCLAD · M · P · XIV

B · R · N · IMPR · CÆSAR · TRAIANA · VENTA · BEL · GARVM · M · P · XV

BONO · RE PUBLICÆ NATO · IMP CÆS · ELA GABALVS · A · SORVI ODVNVM · M · P XIX

IMP · C · ANTON PIVS · P · M · TR · P · PA · PAT · CO II · A CAST · L EC · M · P XX

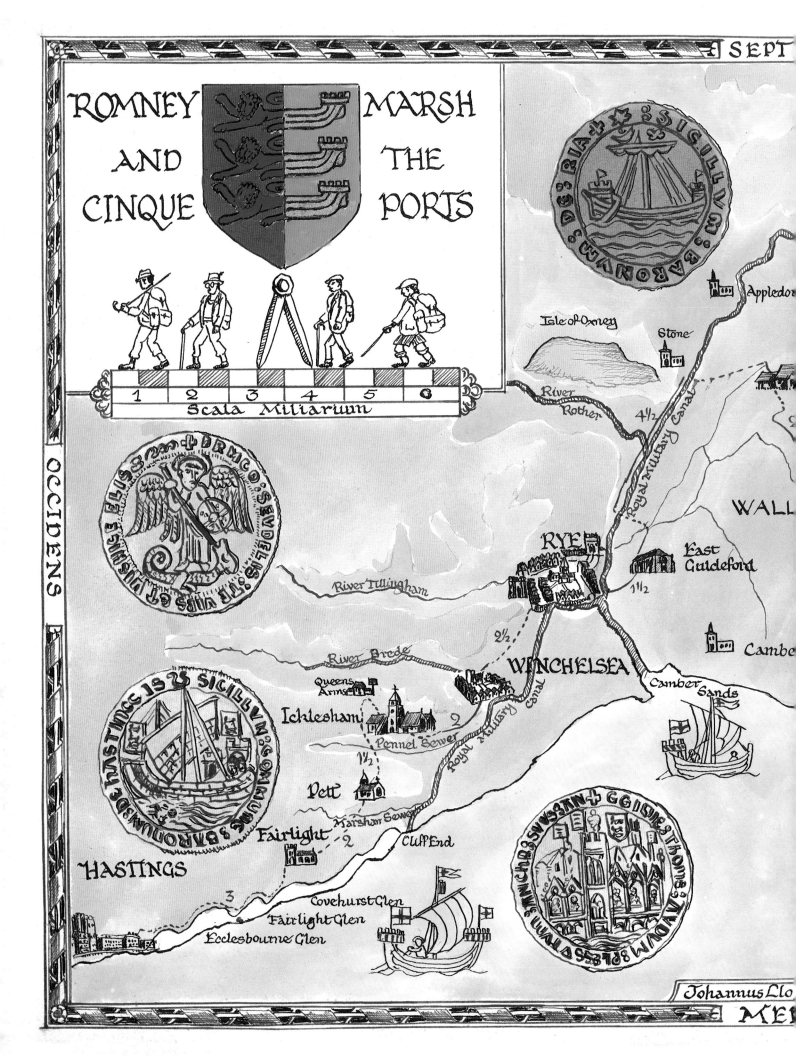

HYTHE

Aldington Hills

Royal Military Canal

PORTUS LEMANIS

West Hythe

Star Inn

3

Burmarsh

1½

ROMNEY MARSH

Newchurch

Snare

Snargate

St Mary in the Marsh

Dymchurch

2

RHEE

Brenzett

Fairfield

Ivychurch

Brookland

WALL

4

Old Romney

2

3½

Littlestone

ND MARSH

Greatstone

SHEPWAY

Ship Inn

NEW ROMNEY

Lydd

Shingle

Shingle

Denge Marsh

Shingle

Dungeness

descriptit.

KEY TO MAP		SEALS	TYPICAL SHIP SERVICE
Cinque Port	RYE	HYTHE	6 Ships
Places on route	Pett	(upper right)	122 Men
Route by road		ROMNEY	4 Ships
Route by path		(lower right)	65 Men
Churches on route	as seen	RYE	9 Ships
Miles between churches	3	(Top – reverse and obverse)	156 Men
Other churches		WINCHELSEA	21 Ships
Other places	Snare	(Bottom – reverse & obverse)	596 Men
Marshland under 50 ft		HASTINGS	5 Ships
Higher land over 50 ft		(Left – reverse & obverse)	96 Men

HEN we walked across the Marsh we soon found the ravelly roads described so well by Kipling. We also found that it is no longer marsh as such, but first class sheep pasture very good to walk on. The fascinating story of the evolution of the marsh and of its influence on the Cinque Ports is told briefly here. Ten thousand years ago these hundred square miles of so-called marsh were under the sea in a shallow bay bounded by the low Aldington Hills and entered by three rivers: the Brede, Tillingham and Rother. These rivers helped to create the marsh by depositing silt when the land underwent cycles of depressions and uplifts. The eastward drift of shingle, which created Dunge-ness assisted the process by forming bars across the River mouths which slowed their flow. During an uplift in Roman times the eastern half of the marsh was raised by this natural means and was saved from further inundation by the great walls of Rhee and Dymchurch. About this time the Rother left its original channel eastward to Hythe for a new course south towards Romney where its estuary created a shallow harbour marked by Greatstone and Littlestone. The other two rivers joined at their mouth to make a natural harbour for Rye and Winchelsea, which stood on its original site south of Rye on a spit of shingle and was called Gwent-chesel-ey. These harbours favoured the growth of four major ports just after the Norman Conquest when traffic and trade with France were increasing. The Portsmen were required to lend fully-manned ships to the King for the defence of the realm. Dover, Hastings and Sandwich also performed similar ship-service thus concentrating our earliest naval resources along a strategic part of the coast. The Confederation of the Cinque Ports which enabled them to organise their ship-service eventually comprised seven Head Ports and more than thirty affiliated towns. In return the Confederation enjoyed and amply deserved such privileges as exemption from taxation, immunity from national jurisdiction and honours at court. At the peak of their power at the turn of the 13th cent: the Cinque Ports fleet was a force to be reckoned with. But the Portsmen forgot the more insidious foe behind them. Their own brothers, the Marshmen were busy reclaiming new innings of land which so reduced the tidal flow at the estuaries that they gradually became silted up. A number of fierce storms in the 13th cent: ~ one of which destroyed Gwent-chesel-ey and diverted the Rother from Romney ~ increasing raids by the French and resort to piracy by the Portsmen combined with the incessant land reclamation to bring about the decline and even demise of the once proud Ports. ❖

In this walk we saw all the Head Ports except Dover and Sandwich. We saw Hythe whose former haven went right up to the Roman fort named after the Limene or Rother; we saw Romney which lost its river in 1287 and is now out of sight of the sea; we walked between Rye and Winchelsea where ships once assembled in the harbour for battle; and last of all we came to Hastings which lost its harbour before the others. The ships had been replaced by sheep and there were signs that sheep were being replaced by potatoes. ❖

Romney Marsh

What better place to meet than at the "Star"
At evening in a comfortable bar?
John, Gerry, Pat and Mick were deep in talk
About the prospects for the coming walk.
Next morning we went up to see the church
Seemingly perched upon the roofs of Hythe –
A church with little space on which to grow,
Nor yet sufficient space for those who'd died:
The chancel floor was raised above the nave
To build an ambulatory beneath,
Which then became a charnel house of fame,
More popular with tourists than the church.

We took Green Lane – how apt! – by the canal,
Where hornbeam leaves lay floating on the pools,
Or lingered yet all golden on the trees.
A seashell in the wall of West Hythe church
Reminded us that this was once the shore.
In Roman times 'twas Limene estuary
Commanded by a fort whose walls are now
Crumbled away or tumbled down the hill.
Portus Lemanis Fort to-day commands
Only the marsh – the harbour is no more.

And now across the level sward we turned
Among the flocks of sheep that safely grazed,
Disturbed by none until we came along,
Nor yet by noise, for wind among the reeds
Was now the only sound that could be heard.
The line of hills that were the coastal cliffs
When all the marsh was underneath the sea
Reduced in height but grew in breadth as though
We'd taken to a boat across the bay,
Or so it seemed, until a port of call –
"Shepherd and Crook" of Burmarsh came in sight,
Bringing our little voyage to an end,
With bread and beer and signals sent by wire
To book accommodation for the night.

We visited the church behind the inn,
And found therein a notice saying thus:
"The eighty homes of Burmarsh are spread o'er
An area of five square miles of marsh,
And this compares with five square miles of town
Which London's railway termini do bound".
A footpath thence on sheep-cropped turf we took;
Larks sang – 'twas like a downland walk, though flat.
Each dike we crossed by bridge in good repair,
The Rural District Council well aware
That footpaths in the Marsh should be maintained.

The Dymchurch organ filled the church with sound.
"Widor," said John, and right enough was he.
She ceased to play – she'd played for thirty years –
And talked to us about her choir of twelve
And of the Friends of Dymchurch and the Fete
And Dr Syn of Russell Thorndike's tales.
While listening, we looked around to see
The chevron mouldings on the chancel arch
And Norman doorways to the tower and porch.

We took a turn upon the Dymchurch Wall,
A mighty Roman monument that keeps
The sea from flooding o'er the land, and which
The Court of Jurisdiction of the Lords
Of Romney Marsh maintained throughout the years
Most diligently, serving all the Marsh.
The Court is there today and in New Hall
The Inland Drainage Board still levies rates
To save the land from the encroaching sea.

In case we were benighted in the marsh
We went by tree-lined lane to one more church
With low grey walls and lichen-coloured roofs
And twisted vane crowning the shingled spire,
Standing amid the fields of darkening dun,
St Mary's in the Marsh at set of sun.
New Romney was our final port of call;
Ships once tied up there to St Nicholas's wall.
There is but one ship in the town today
And that an inn – what better place to stay?

Walland Marsh

From New Romney to Rye
Friday 23rd October 1964

Though Romney's Cinque Port fame has long since gone,
The splendour of her church still lingers on;
The nave and aisles ended in chancels three
To make the church a perfect entity.
The Vicar with a class from school came by
To tell them of their local history,
And doubtless also Christianity.

We reached Old Romney by a grass-grown road –
Maybe the oldest way between the towns –
To find the Church was under scaffolding.
Historic Churches Preservation Trust
Had allocated seven thousand pounds
Towards repairs; amid the mess, the font
With Purbeck marble shafts, an altar too
With consecration crosses there incised,
Which long served in the churchyard as a step.

We crossed the ancient bank known as Rhee Wall,
The proper boundary of Romney Marsh,
And westward went away o'er Walland Marsh
By 'ravelly' lanes and cleared potato fields,
With prints of bird's feet in the drying mud –
A sign that marshland sheep were in decline.
The noon light on the marsh horizon shone
So clear it seemed but one field's breadth away.
The wind blew harder from an icy sky
While snowy wisps of cloud came sailing by.

Beside a bank we sheltered from the wind
Neath swishing stems of teasel, rush and reed;
Then on again towards a railway line.
The notice SE and CR was still
Upon the Mountain Crossing gate ahead –
A name that must have been a joke we thought.
And now deep dikes athwart the Brookland path,
Too wide to cross, deflected us; maybe
These cuts were made by Romney men of old
In a despairing effort to re-guide
The Rother to their "port of stranded pride."

At Brookland it was later than we thought –
It usually is – and so we sought
The nearby inn, wherein the landlady
Sat knitting at the bar and listening
To all our talk but saying naught, no doubt
On warmer days she's settin' at the door:
A Romney Marsh wise woman, to be sure.

The church of St Augustine by the inn
Contained a wealth of curiosities,
Detaining us at least another hour –
The barge boards on the porch, arcades awry,
The famous leaden font all storied round,
The horse-box pews, the tithe-pen and the school;
Nor could we miss the conical bell tower,
Said to have fallen off in sheer surprise
The day a virgin came there as a bride.

Two miles by twisting lane from Brookland church –
'Tis not much more than one as sea-birds fly –
Stands Fairfield church, in fields and girt by dikes
As by a moat; and charmingly restored,
With pulpit, pews and lectern painted white.
The triple-decker's lowest pen seemed most
Inadequate for any ample clerk.
St Thomas church is close to Becket's Barn,
And Becket reclaimed marshland hereabouts
Maybe he named his innings this 'Fairfield'.

The Isle of Oxney stood up from the Marsh
Beyond a sea of deep black waves of plough.
While crossing them, a squall from out the north
Struck suddenly; we sheltered under elms
Until the storm had passed. The sky now clear,
We walked along the Military Canal,
Turning aside to East Guldeford church,
Barnlike and buttressed, built in Tudor brick,
Abandoned-looking in the evening light.
Rye's noble mound rose up against the sun;
Our journey over Romney Marsh was done.

55

East Sussex Coast and Marsh

From Rye to Hastings

Saturday 24th October 1964

The sun appeared upon a frosty morn
To make of Rye a rose red town at dawn,
When our patrol continued on its round
From Landgate to the Ypres Tower whence
The Gungarden look-out espied no French
Nor any bell to ring in Watchbell Street;
Then down Green Steps to where the Strand Gate stood
And Cinque Ports Street where ran the western wall.

Then back to breakfast at the Railway Inn
Where we had slept in one large room for four —
Electric fire and auto tea-machine
And milk et cetera left outside the door.
And now through busy streets all full of cars —
Surely they should be banned from such a town —
On cobbles between tiled or boarded rows,
To see the church, cathedral-like in close.

St Mary's church is paramount but still
Bears stains from fire and pillage by the French,
They stole the bells once during an attack,
But Rye men crossed to France and brought them back.
The quarter-boys above the ancient clock,
Striking their cheerful chimes on gilded bells
Recalled that Time's inevitable shadow
Passeth away; it was now time to go.

Twixt Rye and Winchelsea there runs a path
O'er water meadows but 'tis rarely used.
How strange that local people should neglect
This direct way between the ancient towns.
A green causeway points straight to Winchelsea
And helps to find the bridges o'er the dikes
Look out! A bull is there! Eyes leave the hill;
We lose our bearing on the old black mill.

Gwent-chesel-ey stood on a shingle spit
Until a great storm inundated it.
In fact the townsfolk were prepared for flight
And made at once to Winchelsea's new site
On ninety acres of the Iham Hill,
The streets quartered in Roman fashion still.
A timely and praiseworthy move indeed,
And one in which King Edward took the lead.

We climbed the hill beneath the Pipewell Gate,
But where was Winchelsea among the flowers?
The town seemed just as Patmore saw it, in
"A sunny dream of centuries ago".
The fragment of St Thomas' church that's left –
The nave was either burnt or never built –
Makes one regret that one will never know
The master mason's dream of long ago.

We went out by Winchelsea's old New Gate,
A stone's throw from the Military Canal,
Along a rolling sunny, sandstone ridge
Through apple orchards; so to Icklesham,
Here was the thirteenth church we visited,
And like the others full of interest,
With weeping chancel longer than the nave.
And beautiful yet simple Norman work.

The Queen's Arms was an inn of secret charm
With one long view down River Brede to Rye
And flowers in yellow tubs with door to match,
And white or tile-hung walls – no need of thatch.
Then down we went to cross the Pannel sewer
And up the green slope crowned by Pitt church spire
And down again across the Marsham sewer,
Thence up five hundred feet to Fairlight Tower.

Then John, pneumonia victim recently,
Astonished by his own temerity,
Agreed to walk to Hastings by the cliff
Provided he had an aperitif.
A superb switchback coastal walk was this
By sandy path through bracken, birch and pine;
Each deep declivity well-named a glen –
Covehurst, Fairlight and lastly Ecclesbourne.

At length Pat broke his silence on the way:
He said we'd walked our thousandth mile that day.
But then we knew not in our haste and heat
We'd climbed since lunch at least a thousand feet.
Before we climbed East Hill, the sun had set
And soon the sky with stars all o'er was fret.
We gazed in admiration from the down
Upon the myriad lights of Hastings town.

The End of the
Seventeenth Walk

osse Way and Icknield Way extend throughout the breadth of Britain while Ermine Street and Watling Street nearly run its length. They are known as the four Royal Roads because travellers on them were protected, under the so-called Laws of Edward the Confessor, by the king's peace. The thirteenth century map on the next page shews all four roads intersecting at Dunstable whereas only Icknield Way and Watling Street cross there. It also shows the former going from Salisbury to Bury St. Edmunds. This map was perhaps the origin of the name VIA ICENIANA given to the Salisbury Road in Iter VIII; "Ackling" Dyke may have the same origin. In 1966 we followed the traditional Icknield Way considering it simply as a trackway some 4000 years old connecting west and southwest England with East Anglia. We knew that on Akeman Street and on a long length up to Newmarket from Ickleton it coincided with Roman Roads. What we did not realise was, first, that Icknield Way is really a broad band of parallel tracks and, secondly, that certain sections were straightened out by the Romans, some departing a long way from the traditional route. Encouraged by Ivan Margary, a group of field-workers, calling themselves "the Viatores", have recently formed these conclusions and published their work in a book which emulates Margary's "Roman Ways in the Weald." One of these Roman-engineered sections is the Lower Icknield Way. Its fellow, a hillside track called the Upper Icknield Way was undisturbed. This most beautiful trackway winding along the Chilterns, above the plain but below the hills, strongly reminded us of the Old Road. An old description of it is given overleaf. Beyond the Chilterns right into Norfolk, where the hills are much reduced in height, the Way continues to follow the north facing edge of the chalk as the Old Road followed the south. Icknield Way is better preserved than the Old Road. Pilgrims to Walsingham may have ensured its survival as pilgrims to Canterbury are said to have rescued the Old Road. More probably its use as a cattle drove and its ancient name have helped to identify it and so preserve it. Deeds of adjoining land from earliest times refer to it in many different though similar forms. Moreover, there are places along or near the route with strikingly similar names. Thus we find Ickleford, Ickleton, Icklingham and Ickburgh ~ this last on Iter XIV; Pyrton (nr Watlington) and Pixton (nr Hitchin); Streatley on the Thames and again north of Luton. Within the present century the name "Icknield Way" has been given to new roads in Goring, Luton, Letchworth, Baldock and Thetford. There is even a telephone exchange called Icknield serving the area around Lilley. On Iter I our companion had been Belloc's "Old Road". Now we were guided by a contempory work called the "Icknield Way" by Edward Thomas when it was still regarded as no more than a British trackway. Through seven days and seven counties between Thames and Thetford we followed the Way sometimes choosing our own parallel tracks to avoid long hard roads. If our way was wayward, whether by abandoned railway, disused canal or, fortuitously, by a Romanised alignment to Dunstable, it nonetheless ran the course and connected the Berkshire Ridgeway (Iter VII) with Norfolk (Iter XIV) ~ Avebury with Grimes Graves. Now we know the way by which neolithic man brought his flints to Wessex. We also knew from camps and ditches and reports of many finds on the way that it was used during the next 2000 years at least. No one knows, however, whence the travellers came nor whither they went. There is no beginning or end to the Icknield Way and is "a symbol of mortal things with their beginnings and ends in immortal darkness", as said E. Thomas ·:·

From Ripley
to Sendmarsh

Iter XVIII
One Day

Pyrford Church

Wisley Church

Newark Priory

Ockham Church

Wisley

Inn

Pyrford Lock

Pyrford

Moat

Pyrford Place

Horticultural Gardens

Ockham Mill

A3

Remains of Newark Priory

Paper Court Lock

RIPLEY

Ockham Park

Ockham

Prews Farm

Sendmarsh

A3

Scale: 2" ≈ 1 mile
Based on O.S. 2½" map
Sheet No. TQ 05

Distance walked:
By road   5½ miles
  " path   4½ "
  Total   10 miles

Inspiration for the unique figures in the altar frontal came from a fresco C. 1140 on S. wall of Pyrford Church

Designed by Miss J. Edwards
Embroidered by Capt. G. Colpoys R.N.
Photo'd by J. C. M. Blatch

Altar Frontal at Pyrford Church "The Pilgrims Way"

BY·THE·WAY·

We mustered five upon that day in May
When we enjoyed a walk beside the Wey.
Not unexpectedly there was John Lloyd
Without whose presence there'd have been a void;
But more surprisingly his wife called Pegs,
Came out to show us how to use our legs,
And there was also Bill, a newcomer,
Prepared to walk in winter or summer.
The fourth one as you may have guessed was Pat,
Armed with his trusty Ordnance Survey map,
And last of all but by no means the least
Was Father Smith, a Roman Catholic priest,
Who, though he was near three score years and ten,
Would cheerfully have walked the round again.

After some coffee at a Ripley inn
We were refreshed and ready to begin,
Escaping from the traffic on the road
Through gaily painted gates to an abode
Of utter peace, a memorable place
Called Ockham Park where dwelt Lady Lovelace.
We met her representative who asked
Whether by chance we knew we had trespassed.
Our trespasses were happily forgiven,
So from the lovely park we were not driven.
Instead he pointed out the nearby church
Where Pat did walk a mile for key to search –
It was expedient to take such pains
While having treatment for his bulging veins,
And some instructions from the hospital
To walk each day and not to stand at all.

We gazed upon the chancel's eastern wall
At seven graduated lancets tall,
For which this Ockham church is widely famed;
Than these no finer lancets can be found.
Within the chancel was an early brass
To William Freeland who had said the mass
When Black Death raged; the danger being met
He built the chapel of St Margaret.

Iter XXIII

eyond a lane that ends at Ockham Mill
We crossed some fields where all was quiet and still,
When suddenly a fearful shriek we heard,
Quite foreign to our ears; a mocking bird,
Or maybe mating call of some peacock
Was what we heard that day near Pyrford Lock.
Ere long we came upon the old canal,
Beside the gardens horticultural,
And turned to walk along the towing path;
No barges there – the only thing on draught
Was mild and bitter in the Anchor Inn
For which we had some time been hankering
And very pleasant 'twas to sit down there
While Father Smith took out his book of prayer.

ecause the fields were soaked by recent rain
We went to Wisley by a winding lane,
Near which there was a prehistoric place
Where dwellings with post holes had left a trace
And boys at play beside the river found
An old dug-out canoe beneath the ground.
It seemed that fewer people lived there now
Than dwelt in pits four thousand years ago.

farmer here ploughed up a sarsen stone;
Now it lies over him – his work is done.
Who would not envy him this peaceful place
In which to rest his bones? A little space
Beside the tiny church whose Norman plan
Was hardly altered since it first began.
Behind a red-tiled farm it looked quite fine,
A picture framed beneath a lone Scots pine.

e now retraced our route along the Wey,
Or "Navigation" as 'tis called today.
We crossed a bridge on to the further side
To follow thence an avenue or ride
And then a lane up to some higher ground
Where Pyrford Church stands on an ancient mound
That looks across the level watermeads.
The river here breaks into many leads
Which wind about a ruined priory
Much as they do upstream at Waverley.

t was a lovely church; and like Wisley
Was mostly built in the twelfth century;
And loving hands devoted many hours
Arranging all the pentecostal flowers.
Rosettes and flowers were painted in the roof,
Where once the Rood was raised – sufficient proof,
Said Father Smith, that there was a celure;
Beyond the reach of vandals 'twould endure.

at said "Let's go along the Navigation
To Old Woking and Send – our destination,"
But when we reached the lock called Papercourt,
To our dismay the path which we had sought
Was ankle deep, in fact quite inundated,
As Father Cuthbert amply demonstrated.
Another way was found though in the end,
We walked neither to Woking nor to Send,
Nor even Ripley whence that day we came –
For that the navigator was to blame;
And, lest perhaps that judgement sounds too harsh
Let it be said we finished at Sendmarsh,
Mid 'semis' and the sound of the A3;
So hastened thence by bus back to Ripley.

efore we left we went to see the church,
A cobbled path went up towards the porch
Beneath an avenue of dark yew trees
It didn't seem to be likely to please.
But Ripley church was not a place to burke;
The chancel had the rarest Norman work.
There was a most elaborate string course
Of leaves and flowers; it was a tour de force
Set off by shafts each with a capital;
We wondered at the purpose of it all.

he vicar told of old William, a tramp
Who nightly in the nave would make his camp;
And so God's house ere long became his home,
And he no longer felt the need to roam.
How many priests would show such kindly feeling
For ragged reject from the world sent reeling:
Unfortunately as at nearby Ockham
They like their churches clean, and so they lock 'em!

**The End of the
Twenty-third Walk**

63

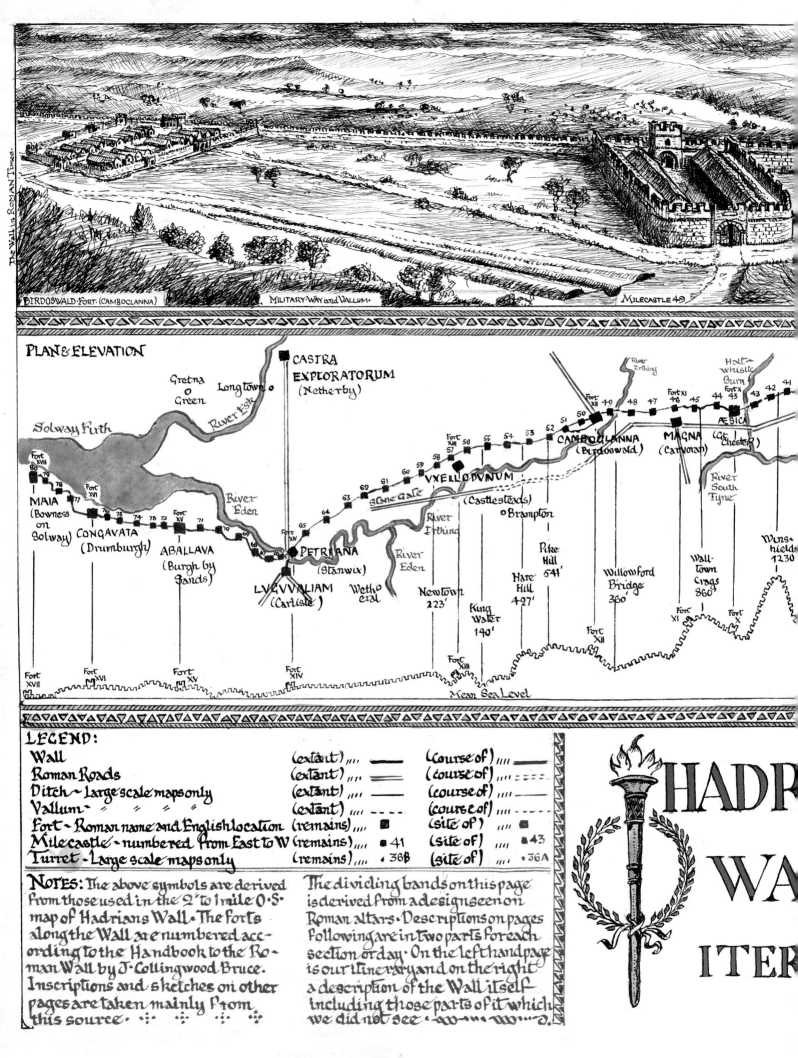

The Wall in Roman Times.

BIRDOSWALD·FORT·(CAMBOGLANNA)   MILITARY·WAY and VALLUM·   MILECASTLE 49·

PLAN & ELEVATION

CASTRA
EXPLORATORUM
(Netherby)

Gretna
o
Green   Longtown o

River Esk

Solway Firth

River Irthing   Halt-
whistle
Burn

Fort
XII 49   48 47   Fort XI
48 45   Fort X
44 43   43 42 41
ÆSICA
51 50

Fort
XVII
80   79
78
Fort
XVI
77
MAIA
(Bowness
on
Solway)   CONGAVATA
(Drumburgh)
76 75   74 73 Fort XV 72   ABALLAVA
(Burgh by
Sands)
71
70
69
68
67 66   65
Fort
XIV   PETRIANA
(Stanwix)
LVGVVALIAM
(Carlisle)   River
Eden

Wetho
ral

River Eden

64
63   62 61
60 59
58
Stone Gate   VXELLODVNVM
(Castlesteads)

Fort
XIII 56 55 54 53 52   CAMBOGLANNA
(Birdoswald)   MAGNA
(Carvoran)

57   o Brampton   (Gt. Chester)

River
Irthing   River
South
Tyne

Newtown
223'   King
Water
140'   Hare
Hill
427'   Pike
Hill
541'   Willowford
Bridge
360'   Walltown
Crags
860'   Winshields
1230

Fort
XIII   Fort
XII   Fort
XI   Fort
X

Fort
XVII   Fort
XVI   Fort
XV   Fort
XIV   Mean Sea Level

LEGEND:

	(extant)		(course of)	
Wall	(extant) ,,,, ———	(course of) ,,,, ———		
Roman Roads	(extant) ,,,, ═══	(course of) ,,,, ─ ─ ─		
Ditch ~ Large scale maps only	(extant) ,,,, ───	(course of) ,,,, ────		
Vallum ~ ,,,, ─ ─ ─	(extant) ,,,, - - - -	(course of) ,,,, - - - -		
Fort ~ Roman name and English location	(remains) ,,,, ◼	(site of) ,,,, ◼		
Milecastle ~ numbered from East to W	(remains) ,,,, ◼ 41	(site of) ,,,, ◼ 43		
Turret ~ Large scale maps only	(remains) ,,,, • 36B	(site of) ,,,, • 36A		

NOTES: The above symbols are derived from those used in the 2" to 1 mile O·S· map of Hadrians Wall· The forts along the Wall are numbered according to the Handbook to the Roman Wall by J·Collingwood Bruce· Inscriptions and sketches on other pages are taken mainly from this source· :·: ·:·

The dividing bands on this page is derived from a design seen on Roman altars· Descriptions on pages following are in two parts for each section or day· On the left hand page is our itinerary and on the right a description of the Wall itself including those parts of it which we did not see· ∞∞∞∞∞∞∞∞∞∞.

HADR
WA
ITER

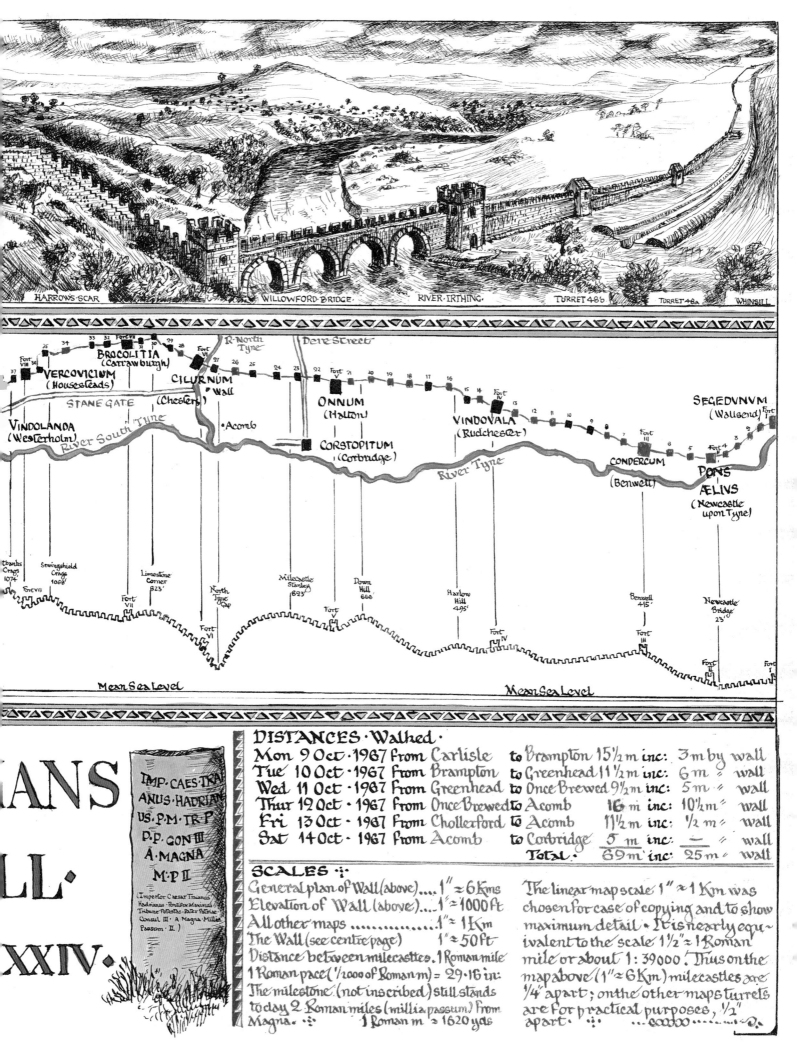

HARROWS·SCAR WILLOWFORD·BRIDGE RIVER·IRTHING TURRET·48b TURRET·48a WHINSILL

Map (centre):

Fort VIII · VERCOVICIUM (Housesteads) · BROCOLITIA (Carrawburgh) · CILURNUM (Chesters) · R·North Tyne · Dere Street · ONNUM (Halton) · Fort V · VINDOVALA (Rudchester) · SEGEDVNVM (Wallsend) Fort · CONDERCUM (Benwell) · PONS ÆLIVS (Newcastle upon Tyne)

STANE·GATE · VINDOLANDA (Westerholm) · River South Tyne · Wall · Acomb · CORSTOPITUM (Corbridge) · River Tyne

37 36 35 34 33 32 31 30 29 28 27 26 25 24 23 22 21 20 19 18 17 16 15 14 13 12 11 10 9 8 7 6 5 4 3 2

Elevation (lower):

Coanks Crags 1074' · Fort VIII · Sewingshield Crags 1088' · Limestone Corner 823' · Fort VII · North Tyne Gap · Fort VI · Milecastle Stanley 1823' · Fort V · Down Hill 668' · Harlow Hill 495' · Fort IV · Benwell 415' · Fort III · Newcastle Bridge 23·0 · Fort II · Fort I

Mean Sea Level   Mean Sea Level

ANS
LL·
XXIV·

DISTANCES · Walked ·

				inc:	by wall
Mon 9 Oct·1967	from Carlisle	to Brampton	15½ m	inc:	3 m by wall
Tue 10 Oct·1967	from Brampton	to Greenhead	11½ m	inc:	6 m " wall
Wed 11 Oct·1967	from Greenhead	to Once Brewed	9½ m	inc:	5 m " wall
Thur 12 Oct·1967	from Once Brewed	to Acomb	16 m	inc:	10½ m " wall
Fri 13 Oct·1967	from Chollerford	to Acomb	11½ m	inc:	½ m " wall
Sat 14 Oct·1967	from Acomb	to Corbridge	5 m	inc:	— " wall
		Total·	69 m	inc:	25 m " wall

SCALES ∴

General plan of Wall (above).... 1″ ≈ 6 Kms
Elevation of Wall (above).... 1″ ≈ 1000 ft
All other maps .... 1″ ≈ 1 Km
The Wall (see centre page) 1″ ≈ 50 ft
Distance between milecastles. 1 Roman mile
1 Roman pace (1/1000 of Roman m) = 29·16 in:
The milestone (not inscribed) still stands
today 2 Roman miles (millia passum) from
Magna· ∴   1 Roman m ≈ 1620 yds

The linear map scale 1″ ≈ 1 Km was
chosen for ease of copying and to show
maximum detail · It is nearly equivalent to the scale 1½″ ≈ 1 Roman
mile or about 1: 39000 · Thus on the
map above (1″ ≈ 6 Km) milecastles are
¼″ apart ; on the other maps turrets
are for practical purposes, ½″
apart · ∴   ....∞∞∞∞.....·

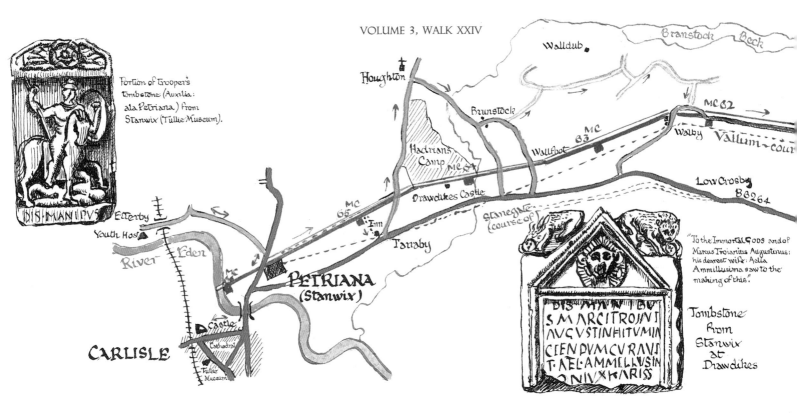

Portion of trooper's tombstone (Auxilia: ala Petriana) from Stanwix (Tullie Museum).

Tombstone from Stanwix at Drawdikes

"To the Immortal Gods and of Marcus Troiarius Augustinus his dearest wife: Aelia Ammillusima saw to the making of this."

The Walk from Carlisle to Brampton

We spent the first night in the Youth Hostel at Etterby near Carlisle. The wind blew and rain lashed outside and it was still raining next morning when we visited the Augustinian cathedral, the only one in the country; some remains of the monastic buildings still exist. In the Tullie Museum nearby were Roman monuments and milestones which were also monuments of a sort because they were often inscribed with the Emperor's name. Re-crossing the River Eden we turned along the line of the Wall at Stanwix Fort fully caped against the steady rain. There were deep pools of water near the site of milecastle 65 and a welcome respite for lunch in the Near Boot Inn at Tarraby. Then we were baulked by the modern Hadrian's Camp and forced northwards to Houghton. At Brunstock we found a good track which soon deteriorated till it became nearly impassable. Near the site of milecastle 62 we regained the line of the Wall and found a lane running with it. Near Wallhead in the hedgebank were four courses of facing stones – our first sight of the actual Wall. At Bleatarn the Vallum and Ditch became visible, the lane turned off and hedgerows marked the course of the Wall across fields to Oldwell.

Luckily as it turned out we diverged to Irthington near the site of milecastle 59. Our hope for tea at the Salutation Inn was realised but there we learned that our route via Newtown to Brampton was cut off by floods at the Irthing bridge – hardly surprising after 1.4" of rain in twenty four hours. So we had to take the longer route via Ruleholme Bridge. After marching the four odd miles in eighty minutes, we arrived in Brampton, put up at the Nag's Head and ended the day with a 'stand-up' fish and chip supper as there were no meals at the inn and no chairs in the fish shop.

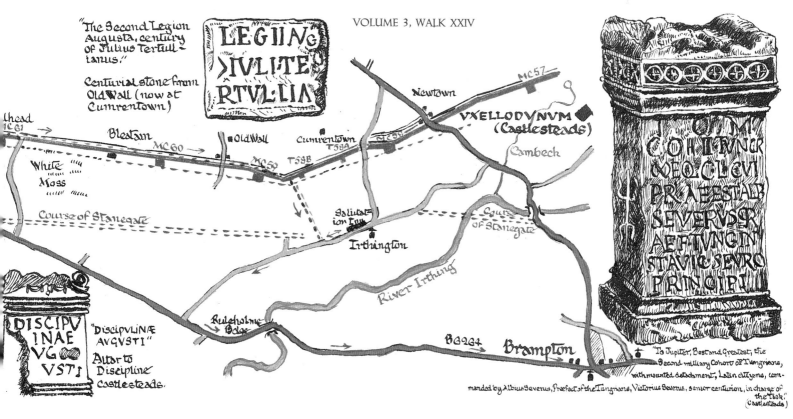

"The Second Legion Augusta, century of Julius Tertullianus."

Centurial stone from Old Wall (now at Cumrentown)

LEG IIAG >IVLITE RTVL·LIA

"DISCIPVLINAE AVGVSTI"

Altar to Discipline Castlesteads.

DISCIPVLINAE AVGVSTI

"To Jupiter, Best and Greatest, the Second milliary Cohort of Tungrians, with mounted detachment, Latin citizens, commanded by Albius Severus, Praefect of the Tungrians, Victorius Severus, senior centurion, in charge of the Task." (Castlesteads)

The Wall from Stanwix to Castlesteads

Stanwix Fort has an advantageous situation on a height above the River Eden, but not much remains of the structure today. It was a large fort probably intended for a cavalry unit one thousand strong (miliaria) which could only have been the 'alae Petriana', which was the Roman name of the fort. Between Stanwix and Castlesteads there is almost nothing to be seen of the Wall. Its line can sometimes be conjectured by a hedgerow or lane or more often by reference to the Ditch on one hand or the Vallum on the other. The Wall is marked by a footpath to Tarraby but soon after that it disappears within the bounds of Hadrian's Camp.

On White Moss the Vallum has four mounds instead of two. This was done by making the ditch above ground because the steep sides might otherwise have collapsed in the marshy soil. From Bleatarn, where the farmhouse lies between the Wall and the Vallum, the works may be easily traced as an old drove-road runs upon the site of the Wall. Beyond milecastle 58, of which there are slight traces, the Wall dips to cross the valley of the Cambeck and is here unprotected from the possibility of attack from the north.

The fort at Castlesteads guards this line of approach. The Roman name VXELL ODVNVM was not in the Notitia List but was obtained from the inscriptions on the Rudge Cup and the Amiens Skillet. Several interesting altars were found here and are preserved on the Castlesteads estate. Among these was the fine altar depicted above with an inscription commemorating a Tungrian cohort composed of Roman citizens entirely; unusual because the Auxilia were not citizens until a qualifying period of army service (twenty-five years) was served. There were relatively few detachments from regular legions employed on the Wall; the main defence was carried by the Auxilia, the majority of which was one thousand cavalry (alae) divided into smaller units of one turmae or about forty-two. Two tombstones, a centurial stone and altar also shown above may be found at some distance from their original site.

Building stone of Catinell vini of Hertfordshire now in out-house at Howgill.

"To the God Cocidius from the soldiers of the XX Legion Valeria Victrix. Aper and Rufus being consuls" *Stonegate* 282-6.

Altar to Cocidius from milecastle 52 now at Lanercost Priory.

The Walk from Brampton to Greenhead

The morning was bright and clear as we walked back towards the Wall through the pleasant grounds of Naworth Park, across the Irthing and so to the Augustine Canon's (Regular) Priory of Lanercost. Built almost entirely of stones from the Wall in 1220 it had suffered severely from raids by the Scots. It is now mainly in ruins except for the nave which is the parish church and which has a very good Early English west front. The Prior's House and Gatehouse still stand. In the vaulted Cellarium beneath the former Refectory is a museum devoted to remains from the Wall. Having rejoined the line of the Wall above Burtholme Beck we met a farmer called Ben Gamble at Hare Hill Farm. We ate our lunch there on a farm cart among the fowls and he provided the tea. He said that, for half-a-crown, he would show us the ten-foot-high section of the Wall alleged to be the highest. In the end we saw it, and an inscription on it, free – he was a generous Yorkshireman! Beyond Banks the going was easy as there was a minor road along the line of the Wall. We saw fourteen courses of stone in turret 52a and the walls of the next two turrets were visible. Pat counted 668 paces between them which is equivalent to nearly two thousand to a Roman mile – the millia passum.

Near the end of the spur and still on the road was Birdoswald fort which contains a farm. There were several good courses visible and the various gates were clearly identifiable. Beyond the fort Mick found an inscription on the fine stretch of Wall on the way to Harrowscar where at milecastle 49 excavation was in progress. Unable to cross the Irthing at the site of Willowford Bridge, we detoured to Gilsland but could see some of the Wall across the river undergoing restoration. In the open rolling grassland after Gilsland we could not in the gathering darkness distinguish between the various linear works. There followed a merry evening at the seedy Greenhead Hotel. A long discussion on why the Tipalt Burn had flooded the school-cellar for years was interrupted at times by demonstrations of poker-jumping by Maurice, a Geordie lorry-driver. We left them to it at 1.00 am.

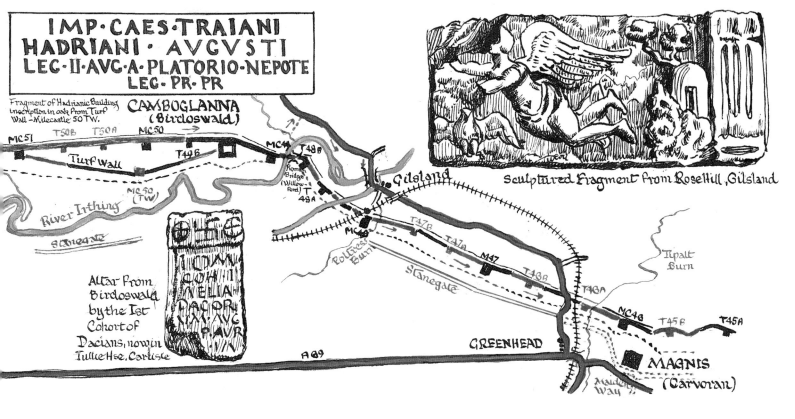

IMP·CAES·TRAIANI
HADRIANI·AVGVSTI
LEC·II·AVG·A·PLATORIO·NEPOTE
LEC·PR·PR

Fragment of Hadrianic Building inscription in oak from Turf Wall – Milecastle 50 TW.

Sculptured fragment from Rosehill, Gilsland

Altar from Birdoswald by the Ist Cohort of Dacians, now in Tullie Hse, Carlisle

CAMBOGLANNA (Birdoswald)

River Irthing

Stanegate

Gilsland

GREENHEAD

MAGNIS (Carvoran)

Tipalt Burn

Maiden Way

The Wall from Castlesteads to Carvoran

Destruction of the Wall is almost complete at the Kingwater but every Roman mile thereafter brings more remains and so more interest. Thus, west of Burtholme Beck there is a section of the Wall nearly seven feet high while at Hare Hill it is nearly ten feet high. The highest ground in this sector is Pike Hill where stood a Roman signal station. Near the river below is the little church of Upper Denton whose tiny chancel arch was built of stones filched from Birdoswald Fort by the Normans. Between milecastle 51 and Birdoswald, the Turf Wall and Vallum run close together both in a good state of preservation. This is the only sector where Turf Wall and Stone Wall are on different lines. The fort of Birdoswald, known to the Romans as Camboglanna meaning "crookbank", stands on a high spur ending at milecastle 49 on Harrowscar where the ground suddenly falls away steeply to the river. The Irthing, having changed its course since Roman times, has left exposed the remains of Willowford Bridge including a massive pier now on dry land. Between the Roman bridge and Gilsland is a fine stretch of Wall close to the river. Turrets 48a and 48b are worth seeing as well as the remains of the bridge.

In the first rolling stretch of Northumberland – the county boundary being on the watershed between the Irthing and the Tyne – the fine linear works, Ditch, Wall, Military Way, Vallum and Stanegate all run close together. The Ditch is particularly impressive being as much as twenty feet high on one side and fifty feet across. After crossing the Tipalt Burn, the Wall rises steeply to Carvoran, a fort which, being separated from the Wall, seems to have as its main function the protection of the crossing of the Stanegate and Maiden Way. The north-west angle tower of the fort can still be seen. Among the varied finds here was a remarkable bucket now in Chester's museum; it was a modius or dry measure made of bronze and in perfect condition.

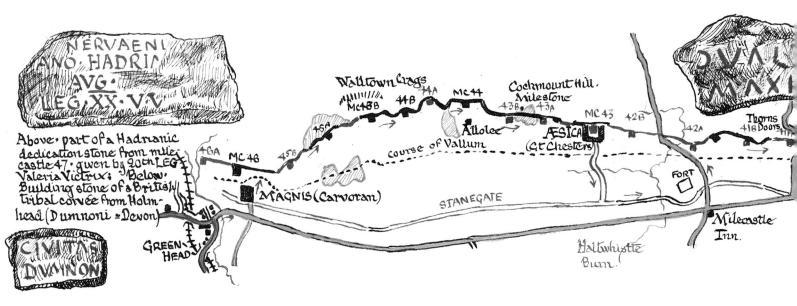

The Walk from Greenhead to Once Brewed

Maurice, the drunken poker-jumper of the previous night, had fled on his lorry long before we rose escaping perhaps from the new Drinking and Driving Act. Passing noisy quarry lorries on our climb up to Carvoran fort, we stood aghast at the destruction of the Wall by quarrying. However penal compensation had forced the owners to finally desist so we were able to enjoy some four hundred yards of Wall before the next quarry. Then steeply up and down the "nicks" we went. From Allolee we saw a great view of the Whin Sill. John said it looked like giant fossilised waves breaking on the moor to the north. At Cockmount Hill we found an uninscribed Roman milestone now serving as a gate-post. In drizzling rain we went on down to Great Chesters or Aesica as it was originally called. It was still well defined with west walls clear to see, an underground vaulted strong-room and a guard-room at the south gate.

At the Milecastle Inn nearby we had a "ploughman's lunch" and a good talk with the landlord. He was a member of a local antiquarian society engaged on filming the Wall. Near the inn was milecastle 42 after which the inn was named. Seven or eight of the eight-feet-thick courses were still standing together with remnants of the gate fastenings. At Thorny Doors we came upon the highest extant piece of Wall, twelve feet high. Excavation is likely to reveal even more courses. We passed over Winshield Crags in steady rain and descended still by the Wall to Peel Gap where we veered south to Once Brewed Youth Hostel.

Being too early for supper, we made a bid to see Chesterholme fort (Vindolanda) but had to turn about at the base of the cylindrical milestone on the Stanegate. The Bognor Guest House provided the evening meal after which we had a few drinks in the Twice Brewed Inn. The warden joined us here with our breakfast which we were to cook ourselves. There were two Americans in the inn who could not find the Wall – being unable to leave their car. We told them we were crazed motorists who had given up cars for Lent.

The Wall from Carvoran to Housesteads

Beyond Carvoran the line of the Wall veers to follow the northward curving line of crags called the Whin Sill, but the Stanegate crosses the country direct to the North Tyne Gap. On Walltown Crags the Wall rises and falls steeply over the Nine Nicks of Thirlwall while holding skilfully to the crags. Then comes a gradual descent all the way to the fort at Great Chesters. The Romans brought water to this fort by an aqueduct from the Caw Burn over five miles away. Remains of a water-mill show that they also used the Haltwhistle Burn. Beside this burn is a small fort which, like Carvoran and Chesterholm, was one of the original Hadrianic forts built apart from the Wall.

In the next sector the Wall crosses another series of gaps between the crags – Thorny Doors, Bloody Gap, Caw Gap and Bogle Hole. At each the Wall enfilades the line of attack and incidentally eases the slope with a re-entrant. After crossing Winshields which is the highest crag on the Wall, a descent is made to Peel Gap and then a further climb by Peel Crag to Castle Nick. For a good view of the awesome basalt columns of Peel Crag, one should go down at Cat Stairs and out a little distance north. Much of the Whin Sill and the man-made works can be seen to advantage from the top of Barcombe Hill, a mile to the south and close to Chesterholm fort.

Beyond Milking Gap the Wall climbs Hotbank Crags over one thousand feet above sea level. From here to the famous fort of Housesteads the wall is continuous and in good condition but, even if it were not, the scenery would be sufficiently rewarding; one prospect looking east from Cuddys Crag is the best known. The length of the Wall described above, about nine miles, is now part of Britain's first long-distance footpath – the Pennine Way. Housesteads, like Roman forts throughout the Empire is standardised on the style of cities. Thus it is rectangular and within the outer defences the area is divided into four by main streets with the command buildings (Praetorium) in the centre.

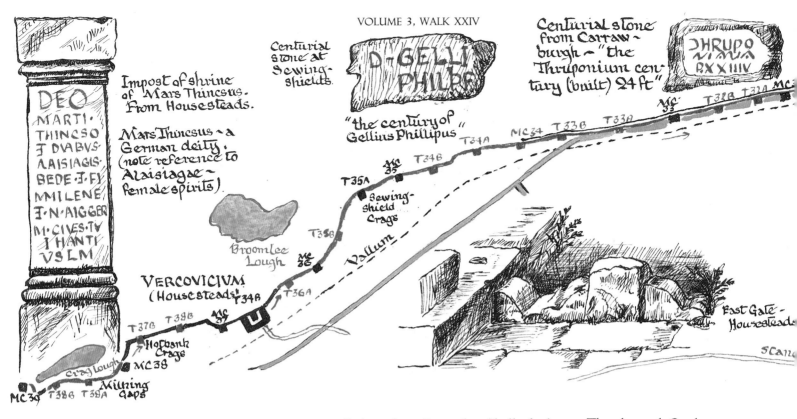

Impost of shrine of Mars Thincsus. from Housesteads.

DEO
MARTI.
THINCSO
J DVABVS
AAISIAGIS
BEDE·J·FI
MMILENE
J·N·AIGGER
M·CIVES·TV
I HANTI
VS LM

Mars Thincsus - a German deity. (note reference to Alaisiagae - female spirits)

Centurial stone at Sewing-shields.

D·GELLI PHILP

"the century of Gellius Phillipus"

Centurial stone from Carraw-burgh - "the Thruponium century (built) 24 ft"

JHRUPO NIMIA RXXIIIV

Broomlee Lough

VERCOVICIVM (Housesteads)

Hotbank Crags

Crag Lough

Milking Gaps

Sewing-shield Crags

Vallum

East Gate - Housesteads

Scale

The Walk from Once Brewed to Chollerford   Thursday 12th October

This was a really lovely day: it was exhilarating to walk along the top of the best part of the Wall. There were remains of barracks at milecastle 39. We sat high up among pine trees looking down at the wild ducks and swans on Crag Lough. Milking Gap was noisy with lowing cattle. We climbed again past milecastle 38 to Hotbank Crags and beyond to milecastle 37 which was the best we had seen so far. Close by was Housesteads where we ate a packed lunch in the museum. Housesteads was the first well-defined fort on our route and in the care of the Ministry of Works. The layout was plain to see: gates with guard-houses, barracks, granaries, remains of the Praetorium and a fine example of a fort latrine. The bath-houses in the Vicus outside the fort had not yet been excavated.

Reluctantly leaving this site we went on over Sewingshields. Beyond a clump of trees we rejoined the road leaving behind the splendid Whin Sill. On the way past Carraw Farm, John pointed out that it had been a Grange of Hexham Priory. Leaving the road for some soggy fields we prospected for Coventina's Well, dedicated to a Celtic goddess. After sinking up to our knees we realised we had been standing in the Well apparently without the blessing of the deity. Adjacent was Carrawburgh fort but little work has been carried out here although the outline of the walls is well pronounced. The most interesting site here was the well-preserved Mithraeum. Facsimile altars are in place with an aperture for lighting them at the back. We read the donative inscriptions. There was one relating to Simplex Simplicianus, a praetor of a unit in the fort. It was 6.00 pm when we left Carrawburgh, and only the half-way point had been reached. Naturally we remained on the road though it would have been more interesting to follow the Vallum, especially at Limestone Corner where we could make out the huge stones abandoned in it. At 7.30 pm we arrived at "The George" at Chollerford but were disappointed in our hopes of refreshment. It was too splendid and expensive for us.

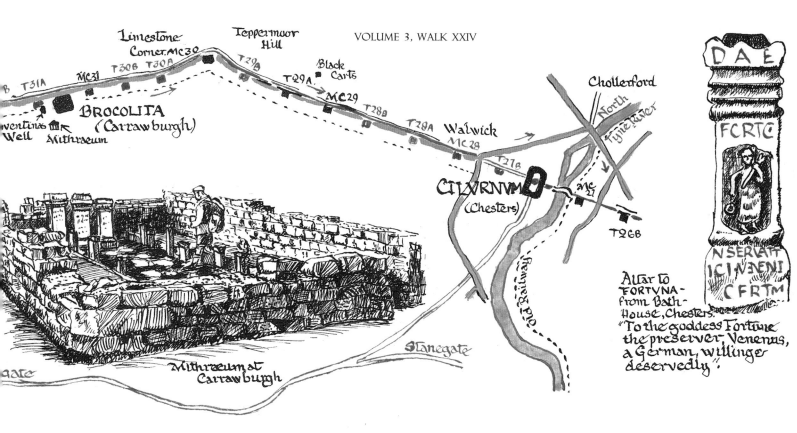

Labels on map: Limestone Corner MC30, Teppermoor Hill, T30B, T30A, T29B, Black Carts, MC29, T29A, T28B, T28A, Walwick, MC28, T27B, CILVRNVM (Chesters), MC27, T26B, Chollerford, North Tyne River, Old Railway, Stanegate, BROCOLITA (Carrawburgh), Coventina's Well, Mithraeum, MC31, T31A, B, gate, Mithraeum at Carrawburgh

Altar illustration: D A E / F C R T O / N SER LATI / ICI VENI / C FRTM — "Altar to FORTVNA from Bath-House, Chesters. 'To the goddess Fortune the preserver, Venenus, a German, willingly deservedly'."

The Wall from Housesteads to Chesters.

A short distance from Housesteads there is a gate through the Wall; it is the only one known other than at a fort or milecastle, and is thought to have been used as a frontier control point. After Kings Hill is the well-known Busy Gap supposed to have been used by the Free-booters in the Middle Ages. Then the Wall mounts for the third and last time over one thousand feet to Sewingshields where milecastle 35 has been much robbed for repairs to a farm-house. The Wall, now not much in evidence, runs down to join the modern road and Vallum which henceforth it accompanies closely all the way to the North Tyne river. Both Vallum and Ditch can be clearly seen. The main place of interest in this section is Carrawburgh fort with the nearby Mithraeum and Coventina's Well.

The Wall now begins to climb once more to the summit called Limestone Corner. Here the Ditch and Vallum have been cut through the hard quartz dolomite. Huge masses of tough excavated stone lie upon the brink. Other pieces each weighing several tons still lie where they were broken in the Ditch. They were never removed though the holes intended for insertion of wedges can still be seen.

On the way down to Chesters there is a fine length of Wall which includes turret 29a at Black Carts north of the road. There the modern road runs upon the Wall which used to show through until the macadam was laid. The Wall then enters the grounds of Chesters House showing four courses of facing stones. The fort of Chesters, known to the Romans as CILVRNVM, was garrisoned by the Second Alae of Asturians, five hundred strong. It guards the bridge across the North Tyne. With Housesteads it is probably the most interesting and most visited of all the forts.

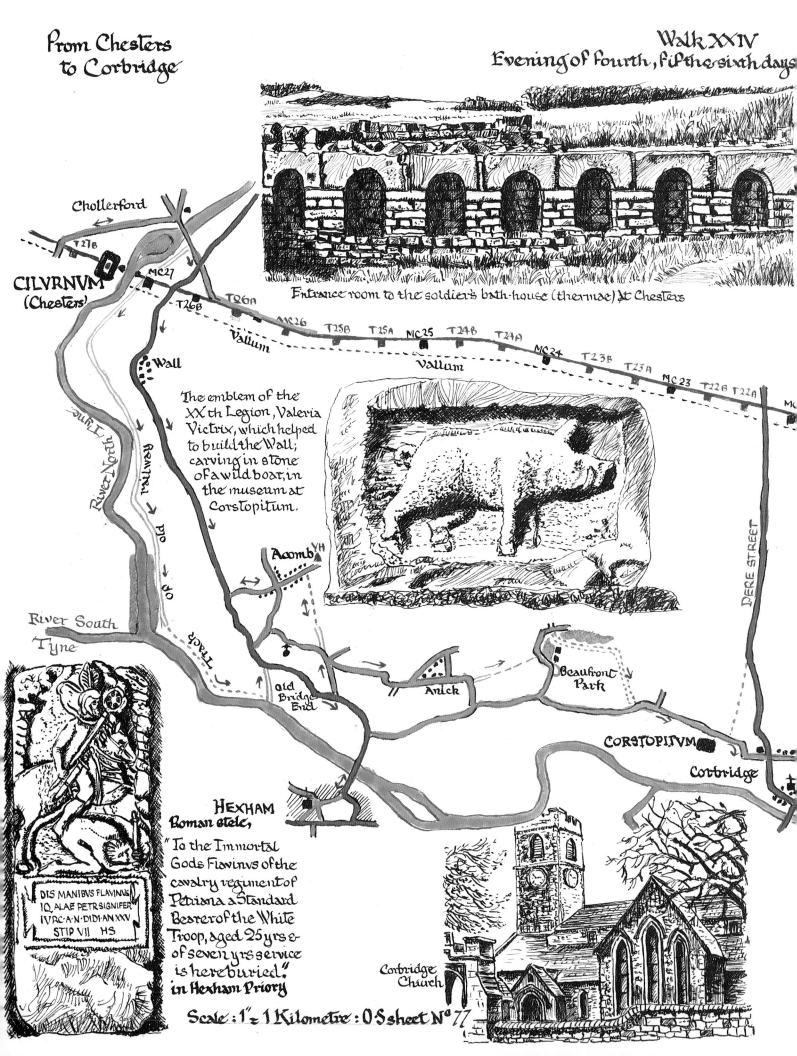

Chollerford

T27B

CILVRNVM
(Chesters)

MC27

T26B   T26A   MC26   T25B   T25A   MC25   T24B   T24A   MC24   T23B   T23A   MC23   T22B   T22A

Vallum

Vallum

Wall

River North Tyne

Railway

old

of

Track

Entrance room to the soldier's bath-house (thermae) at Chesters

The emblem of the XXth Legion, Valeria Victrix, which helped to build the Wall; carving in stone of a wild boar, in the museum at Corstopitum.

Acomb YH

DERE STREET

River South Tyne

Track

Old Bridge End

Anick

Beaufront Park

CORSTOPIVM

Corbridge

HEXHAM
Roman stele,
"To the Immortal Gods Flavinus of the cavalry regiment of Petriana a Standard Bearer of the White Troop, aged 25 yrs & of seven yrs service is here buried."
in Hexham Priory

DIS MANIBVS FLAVINVS
IQ. ALAE PETR SIGNIFER
IVRC·A·N·DIDI·AN·XXV
STIP VII   HS

Corbridge Church

Scale : 1" = 1 Kilometre : O S sheet No 77

Chollerford to Acomb

From Chollerford we turned south on the long road to Acomb and tried for a meal at the Hadrian Hotel at Wall. The lowest price (in full dress) was 15/-. Pity moved a bar-maid to conjure up a "life-saver" in the public bar – to each on a tray scampi, chips, bread and coffee for 10/-. It was 10.00 pm when we reached Acomb, and sought out the warden, who was in the Sun Inn. He led us like horses to our stable for such the Youth Hostel had once been. We passed a fish shop in full cry and noted it.

The North Tyne Gap

We would return to Acomb for a second night so we enjoyed a pack-free day visiting Chesters and Hexham. We made a hasty breakfast and caught a bus back to Chollerford then going back by a footpath to see the remains of the Roman bridge. There were huge abutments where the Tyne used to flow and signs of a former watermill. On the opposite bank of the river, reached a long way round via Chollerford, was the former cavalry fort of Chesters with stable and barracks sites. Better defined were the remains of the Headquarters building and a good example of the comforts in the residence of the Praefectus Equitum, bath houses and hypocaust. Almost intact was the vault of the Legionary strong-room. Outside were the best extant remains of a Thermae or bath house, carefully laid out. There was an abandoned railway line leading by the river direct to Hexham. For several miles it afforded good going on soft grass. We passed an abandoned pit with a picturesque slag-heap. But the final bridge across the river was missing and we had to go a long way round. In Hexham we had a good dinner in a cafe and went into the priory, another Augustinian House where Roman stones had been freely used without any significance. In the south transept there was a complete stele of a Signifer of Auxilia (cavalry), one Flavinus, and other memorials used as "fill-in" materials. We went down steps into an ancient cell under the priory which displayed many pieces of Roman masonry. There was a night-stair still intact together with the candle-shelf at the top. We took great pleasure in walking down the steps into the choir as did Augustinian religious in past centuries for Midnight Office (Matins and Lauds). But there was little left of the monastic buildings.

We had tea at the cafe where we had already eaten and walked pleasantly back to Acomb by lanes and a short path. We collected fish and chips from the shop noted last evening and joined Mr Outside, the warden in the Sun Inn. He was an interesting character, well over seventy and the oldest Youth Hostel warden in the country. He had been a miner for over fifty years but enjoyed his new found contacts with young people from all over the world. He was more active than us. He played darts while we sat and reflected that this had been our hundredth day since our first walk fourteen years before.

Acomb to Corbridge and Newcastle *Saturday 14th October*

We left before 8.00 am – never before had we performed this feat- and followed a high terrace eastward above the Tyne in a howling gale which Mick said was force 8. Driving hard and mostly following lanes, our target was to reach Corstopitum (Corbridge) by opening time at 9.30 am. We did in fact arrive with the Ministry of Works keeper after a pleasant walk through Beaufront Park. Fortunately a good museum provided shelter from the heavy rain. We saw many inscribed stones, Roman army weapons and tools including a pilum shank and entrenching tool whose design was precisely the same as those used today. Even under sheets of rain, the site of this fort is the nearest thing in Britain to Pompeii. It was an arsenal and strategically served the crossing of Stanegate and Dere Street. From the remains of the workshops, pottery and granaries it was plainly a supply base for the Wall garrison as a whole.

Corbridge church, a short distance from the fort, was also of some interest. It contained a great Roman arch in the tower, pillaged from Corstopitum. Adjacent to the church was a defensive tower, built against the Scots raiders. The rest of the wall to Newcastle was viewed from the top of a 'bus. It was not a satisfactory way of seeing it but we did glimpse Dunton Turret and some lengths of wall at Benwell. Reaching Newcastle in time for lunch we made a lightning tour of the Society of Antiquaries Museum admiring especially the scale model of the Wall and the re-construction of the Carrawburgh Mithraeum. Later, on the the afternoon train to King's Cross, these things inspired John to plan the construction of a turret in his garden. We were also inspired to purchase a copy of Bruce Collingwood's "Handbook to the Roman Wall". A Suitable dedication altar was drawn by John in the fly-leaf. We must acknowledge our indebtedness to this book – the source of many of the drawings – but certainly not the one below!

The End of the Twenty-fourth Walk

Overheard at Carrawburgh: "Coventina's Well should be somewhere around here, you chaps"!

At first sight the landscape of Dorset seems a jumble of hills isolated one from another. In fact there is a continuous ridge or backbone through the county from Shaftesbury to Lyme Regis. It is broken only by the River Stour near Blandford and it forms a watershed between the rivers which flow south into the English Channel and those which flow north into the Bristol Channel. The entire ridge extending beyond Dorset to Axmouth is traversed by Britain's oldest and longest trackway, the Great Ridgeway. Together with the Icknield Way, it enabled our earliest ancestors to make a high dry passage of over two hundred and fifty miles from the North Sea near the Wash to the Channel coast. It is probably significant that the Roman Road, the Fosse Way, also ended at Axmouth maybe because it had a good harbour in those days. But neither the Fosse Way nor the Great Ridgeway can be traced to the rivermouth today because of the landslips which have ocurred on the east side of the estuary ⁘

We began our walk of five days at Axmouth in Devon and entered Dorset after a few miles along the coast. Thereafter, except where it has been made a public highway, we followed the Great Ridgeway as far as possible throughout the county. Sometimes we took the alternative so-called 'summer-routes'; these are tracks favoured in dry weather, though below the ridge, they afforded equally good going. During the second third and fourth days we walked upon the Dorset Heights either on or close to the Ridgeway except for a diversion to Sherborne. On the last day where the Ridgeway turns north to Shaftesbury we left it to go on towards Salisbury ⁛⁛⁛

I N the preface to Volume III we looked back over the miles counting them like so many milestones. Now it would perhaps be as well to look forward. As we are four years in arrears with our records the twentieth year is almost upon us so we will look ahead to the second twenty year period ~ up to 1993. By that time, if we are still alive, we will except for Bill be in our seventies. By that time one or more of us may have fallen by the wayside or begun to "babble of green fields." Therefore as we grow older we will look upon each day like St. Augustine as a special day full of significance as if it were the last. It may seem strange that we should feel like this when, so to speak, our journey may be half completed. But when it is considered that our walks occupy only about a week in each year, it sometimes seems as if our allotted span has been reduced from seventy years to as many weeks so that the end seems closer and clearer. ❧ We have joked in the past about becoming automated with motorised sticks or steam gaiters. We have even talked lightly about walking in a special car without a floor, sheltered from the rain and coasting down the hills maybe. We have not until now considered what an "armchair" walker might do. Suddenly deprived of the use of his legs, temporarily or otherwise, with his maps and his memories before him, it is perhaps worth wondering where his armchair ramblings might take him. Probably he would look beyond the Home Counties, the scene of so many past walks. Considering the pleasure of long linear walks he might study the dozen or so leaflets on long-distance footpaths put out by the Countryside Commission. Some of these like Offa's Dyke and the Pembroke Coast Path would be more than a hundred miles long, a prospect which, from the depths of an armchair, he would relish. ❧

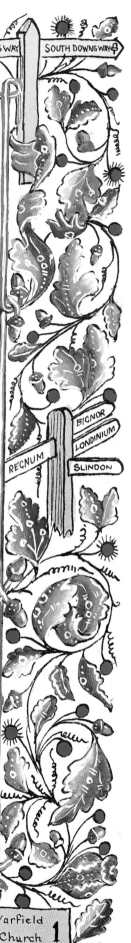

Then he might turn to the other linear walks ~ the many un-
metalled Roman Roads, that obscure track through the centre
of England called the Jurassic Way, the Wansdyke in Wiltshire, canals
and superb river valleys, an increasing number of well matured abandoned railways and hopefully even disused motorways. As if these
were not enough there are whole regions crying out for a visit ~
Quantock, Mendip, Cotswold, the Felden of Warwickshire or the Weald
of Kent. Truly England's variety is inexhaustible. Still sunk in a rev-
erie like poor Susan in Lothbury, visions would arise before him of uncomplet-
ed endeavours and walks so good that they should be repeated. Thus he
might recall how on the first tier we had resolved to walk the Hard Way
to its origin in Wessex, on the fourth to complete the journey of the Four
Men, on the seventh to walk the North Hants Trackway (in dry weather),
more recently to walk along Hadrian's Wall once more and on the eighth
how, on Val's last day, we had glimpsed an enticing ancient downland
up the Winterbourne valley in the solitary heartland of Dorset. ❖ ❖

Then leaping up and and taking pencil and paper he would furiously
write and, calling his able-bodied friends, would present them
with a plan saying, "Now, look here! Go out and do all these things and
since I cannot come with you, return afterwards and tell me all that
occurred." What he wrote will be written down again at the end of
this volume so that, if, through some mischance, our records come suddenly to an end, the reader also will have some notion of our plans
during the next twenty years. These are the signposts which point the
way ahead. There is nothing so good as a signpost to create anticipation.
To the rambler young and old it speaks of new country, undiscovered
and unexplored by him at least. ⋰ ⋰ ⋰ ⋰ ⋰ ⋰ ⋰ ❖

Conservationists say that small is beautiful. It was its smallness that first attracted us to Rutland, also its population density which is the least of all English counties except Westmorland. Then it is said to contain more churches to the square mile than any other county. This alone would suffice to persuade us to go there. So we made a church-crawl to Oakham and Uppingham from the convenient gateway town of Stamford which lies beyond its boundary. Rutland's motto Multum in Parvo tells us that it has many other qualities. It is strange that agriculture should be almost the only industry in a Midland county. The only tall chimney we saw was at Ketton cement works. Many of the villages are stone built, sometimes in stone of different colours. The more common stone is the grey oolitic limestone better known in the Cotswolds. This can be seen in Rutland in alternate courses with a warm brown ironstone.

Throughout Rutland the roads run between hedges so wide apart that the grass verges are often as wide as the road itself, a feature which we had noticed in 1963 in North West Norfolk. It seems that the hedges were so spaced during the enclosures of the late eighteenth century to allow winter traffic to make detours around mud. In the nineteenth century and during earlier part generally, macadam was laid for the first time in a narrow strip leaving broad grass verges. Thus we had grass to walk on when following a road. This was fortunate because many fields were impossible to cross. They were mud traps covered by a thick layer of fine dry silt. Walking more by road than by path enabled us to see about half the fifty villages of Rutland and of course the churches.

Our final impression was of the slogans which we saw here and there and of the stories behind them. There were two main themes. Thus "D'ont flood Rutland" and "Keep Rutland dry condemned a proposal to create a large new reservoir near Empingham on the River Gwash to serve the growing towns of Corby, Peterborough and Wellingborough. Though it will have a water area about the same as Lake Windermere's and will be the largest man-made lake in England, it is some comfort to know that no villages will be drowned.

Other slogans like "Keep Local Government local" and "Hands off Rutland" referred to a plan to absorb Rutland into Leicestershire and so to destroy its county status. "Get the Ruddling habit" was a third more positive theme of less significance to all but devotees of beer and small breweries. Provided Ruddles of Langham are not absorbed by another brewery all will not be lost.

ENVOI

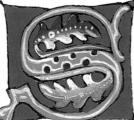

Sadly, like a minority struggling for independence Rutland has lost its two main fights. We are informed by Mr. J. Simmonds, Chief Education officer of Rutland County Council, that by 1976 the heart of this tiny county will be under water. Furthermore this preface is being written on the last day of its existence as a separate County — the last day of March 1974. We may console ourselves that Rutland, formerly Roteland, part of the dowry of the Queens of England, one of whom Edward the Confessor's Queen, gave her name to Edith Weston, will live on albeit as a district rather than a County.

First Day   **Around Stamford**   *Monday 17th March 1969*

St Mary's Church. Stamford.

As John, Pat, Mick and Bill sped northwards on the 9.00 am train from King's Cross to Peterborough dark clouds gathered. When we changed for Stamford it was raining and it rained for the rest of the day with cold north-east winds.

Leaving our kit at the Queens Head we first visited two of Stamford's six parish churches – St Mary's and All Saints. The former is the "mother" church and possesses a very fine Early English tower with a Decorated spire. Features of the latter are exquisite Early English external arcading and an interesting collection of memorial brasses. William Stukeley, the eighteenth-century antiquarian, was vicar here.

Following a typical Rutland lane with broad grass verges we went northwards to Ryhall where we enjoyed excellent Melbourne Ales at the Green Dragon. The pub had a very fine 14th-century undercroft which was used for a beer cellar. John guessed correctly it was once part of a mediaeval manor house. At Ryhall church there was a funeral; the vicar said it was the fourteenth in three months. In the church is the hermitage cell of St Tybba complete with a slit window. Leaving Ryhall by a fine beech avenue we tried to reach Tolethorpe beside the River Gwash but met appalling mud. John carried a shrub as well as a load of mud on his shoes and Bill suggested slapping a tree preservation order on him!

All Saints Church. Stamford.

We came to Little Casterton, a delightfully situated church beside the river with daffodils, snowdrops and celandines growing around it. There was a beautiful brass to Sir Thomas Burton, who died in 1381, and his wife who died a few years later. There was also a pre-Reformation stone altar with three incised crosses in the north aisle. It was a small low grey church with bell-cote. We continued by lanes to Great Casterton which lies on Ermine Street and is the site of a Roman town. There is Saxon "long and short" work at the south-east corner of the church which is largely unrestored. There is also a fine square Norman font with incised patterns of diagonal lines. John Clare the poet was married in this church.

St John's Church Ryhall

We were grateful to find a café for a cup of tea on such a damp evening. Then we followed the main road back to Stamford where, later in the evening, we heard the mid-Lent Fair in the town centre. But we were too tired to go there. Instead we went early to bed at the Queens Head.

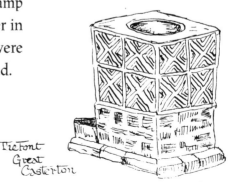

Tie Font
Great
Casterton

Second Day **Stamford To Oakham** *Tuesday 18th March 1969*

St Georges Church. Stamford

e first made a morning tour of Stamford visiting St George's church which was severely damaged by fire in the 13th century. Then we saw the ruined St Leonard's Priory reconstructed c.1110. The north arcade of this former Benedictine House still stands together with a very fine west front reminiscent of Castle Acre Priory. We went on by the 14th-century gateway of the former Friary of Whitefriars (Carmelites) and visited William Browne's Hospital which was founded for ten old men c.1483. The warden gave us a conducted tour. The hospital forms a quadrangle around a lovely old lawn. The chapel retains its ancient rood screen and misericord stall seats. There is a cope stool so that the priest could sit down without creasing his vestments. There is also the original pre-Reformation altar stone with five incised crosses. Fifteen men now live in the hospital as though in the Middle Ages but with all modern conveniences.

St. Leonard's Priory. Stamford.

We left Stamford along Ermine Street, the agger of which was clearly visible in a field to the left, the modern road having diverged to pass through Stamford. Reaching Great Casterton we were glad to escape from the rain for lunch at the "Crown". We then followed the A1 northward and turned off for Tickencote where we saw the famous Norman church with its remarkable chancel arch. It has six orders of moulding each carved with a different design. The other glory of this church is the vaulted chancel also of early Norman date and having a rare feature, a Norman boss.

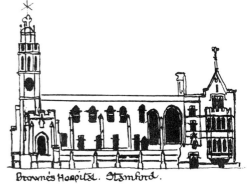

Browne's Hospital. Stamford.

Turning away from the noise of the A1 we followed the river Gwash upstream being lucky to find amid all the mud and rain a hard concrete farm road. Soon after we followed a long drive through Normanton Park where snowdrops and aconites made a welcome pattern of white and yellow among the trees. Edith Weston just beyond the park has an RAF garrison church, much restored but with traces of Norman work. Then a good track for two miles up the Gwash valley brought us to Nether Hambleton whence we followed metalled lanes past Egleton to the main road between Oakham and Uppingham.

Thankfully we found a fish and chip bar in Oakham but accommodation for the night was much more difficult. We tried every hotel and inn that looked cheaper than the "Crown" and gained the distinct impression that we were not wanted. So we returned to the "Crown" and despite the cost were thankful to be out of the rain which had persisted all day.

The Font.
Tickencote.

83

Third Day **Oakham to Uppingham** *Wednesday 19th March 1969*

All Saints Church. Oakham.

We first visited Oakham church which has a magnificent tower and spire dominating the surrounding countryside. The castellated capitals in the nave are a feature of Rutland churches. There is a Norman font c.1180 and a Vulgate (Latin Bible) written on vellum c.1200. With Mr Laxton the caretaker we visited the Norman banqueting hall said to be the most perfect specimen of 12th-century domestic architecture in the country. There are 218 horseshoes on the walls, the result of an ancient custom whereby every peer on first passing through the town should leave a shoe from his horse, or money to have one made, to be hung in the Great Hall. Pat didn't hang his shoe up, but he had to visit the cobbler to have his heels mended. Finally Mr Laxton took us to the County Council offices to get us a guide-book. He was a most helpful gentleman.

The Norman Hall. Oakham.

We crossed the fields to Egleton where Mick was able to take his first photograph. The church was locked but the elaborate late Norman tympanum over the south door was worth seeing. We continued over the railway westward by a good track rising to over five hundred feet, with deep snow near the top. Descending to Brooke we looked at the church which was an unusual restoration of 1597. But there was no inn, and we went on to Braunston to eat at the Blue Ball. All Saints church contains a very late brass of 1596 with an English inscription, "As I was so are ye and as I am so shall ye be", hackneyed perhaps but worth recording once. The green roads and fields to the south were very wet but we progressed past Priors Coppice and Leigh Lodge over higher country close to the Leicestershire border. At Belton the landlord of the Black Horse refused to make tea for us. The church stands on the hilltop and has an interesting 13th-century font with pointed transitional arcading. It is said to have been thrown into a field by Cromwell's men and used as a drinking trough.

St Edmund's Church Egleton.

At last we turned along the road from Leicester to Uppingham leaving it only for half a mile to see the church of St Botolph at Wardley with a small aisless interior, plain enough though the pews and pulpit were painted blue. In Uppingham we arranged to stay at the Central Hotel opposite the famous school. Then we found a fish and chip shop but ordered something better at the "Crown" for tomorrow night.

All Saints Church. Braunston.

North porch and parvise – Stoke Dry.

Fourth Day   **Around Uppingham**   *Thursday 20th March 1969*

he two dear old ladies who kept the Central Hotel were worried about our appearance. As we sat by the stairs we overheard the following conversation:-

First old lady: "Have the troops gone out yet?"

Second old lady: "I think so. They're funny men aren't they?"

First old lady   "Yes and one of them has a blue face."

Second old lady   "But they do keep the stairs clean, don't they?"

First old lady   "I think they'll be alright – if they come back."

This last remark referred to their hope that we would return for a second night. We took one pack between us, bought bread, butter and Leicestershire cheese and left the town by the Stockerston Road. At the top of Kings Hill, over five hundred feet high, we left the road by a good track southwards and came to the Eyebrook Reservoir whence we ascended to Stoke Dry. The clouds had lifted and the ground was beginning to dry out a little.

In Stoke Dry church we found the south aisle under repair. We climbed the scaffolding and talked to Mr May, a carpenter. He was making scarf joints in repairing the roof timbers. All the work was being done by hand and the sawing of one beam would take hours. There was a fine parvise over the north porch, a little room seven feet by eight feet which we went into. The 15th-century rood screen was very much in need of repair. A mile or so away by lanes was Lyddington where there is a large church having a fine three seat sedilia of the Decorated period. In the chancel there are some acoustic jars of earthenware. The Bishops of Lincoln founded a palace here in the 13th century It is next to the church and, because it became an almshouse in 1602, it is known as the Bede House.[1] The Great Hall has a fine timbered roof and original windows including a beautiful oriel window. For some years past the Ministry of Works has been restoring the fabric. We talked to Mr Speechley who was engaged in carving a cornice in green oak and superb detail. He was paid 6d an hour extra for his wood-carving skill.

Lyddington Church

Garden Tower of Bede House, LYDDINGTON

After a meal and drink at the White Hart, an inn with a very homely atmosphere, we crossed several fields to Seaton where we looked at the church. There is a fine Early English chancel with three seat sedilia and canopied piscina, and a very interesting collection of eight consecration crosses mounted in the west wall of the south porch.

17cent Farmhouse at Lyddington

[1] Bede – from pre-Reformation term relating to inmates of monastic almshouses called Beadsmen or women from the Rosary beads carried

aking lanes northwards we crossed the disused branch railway line from Uppingham and came to the top of the hill at Glaston. Calling at the Monckton Arms for tea we were made very welcome. The lady made us sit by the fire, poured the tea herself and demanded to know where we had been – as if we shouldn't have! St Andrew's church was worth a visit. It has a central tower but no transepts.

In the evening light we now followed lanes and tracks westwards to Ayston, a lovely stone village with broad grass verges outside the cottages. There was some good 15th-century heraldic glass in the south aisle of the church. By footpath we returned to the main road and Uppingham where we made for the Crown Inn. There in the comfortable snug we had steak pie, beans and mash and then returned to our beds at the Central Hotel.

Ayston Church

The Crown Inn. Uppingham.

Last Day **Uppingham to Stamford** *Friday 21st March 1969*

o make certain of catching the 17.45 pm train from Stamford we had planned how long we should spend in the various churches we hoped to visit, six in all. It was in many respects the most enjoyable day of the walk, mainly because it remained dry and the sun broke through at midday – the first time we had seen it all week. From Uppingham we followed the track of the disused railway line for two hours. A falling gradient averaging 1-50, or about one hundred feet per mile, made the going easy. Mick was photographed beside an old gradient post marked 1-60. Pat's heel was loose; he hammered it on with a stone but finally lost it in a stream beneath the Seaton viaduct, a huge brick structure carrying the Corby-Oakham line across the Welland valley. Turning north on to the former Rugby-Stamford railway line we proceeded cautiously through Morcott Tunnel, and then climbed up an embankment into the village. The church has a large stone spire and is the most complete Norman church in Rutland. Of particular beauty was the Norman tower arch with three plain orders and elaborately carved capitals.

Permanent Way hut near Seaton

Following lanes eastwards we came to Barrowden, an ancient straggly place with several rough connected village greens. The church is large but much restored. In it was a reference to "rush-bearing", that is the strewing of rushes on the floor. In the Exeter Arms at lunch-time Pat packed the inside of his offending shoe with half beer mats as the nails were coming through. There were no rushes to be had.

Morcott Tunnel

Then we crossed fields, with wide views across the Welland valley into Northamptonshire, and came to the lonely church of St Luke at Tixover. Unhappily it was locked but we noted the fine Norman tower of c.1140, with zig-zag carving on the lower south window and good tympanum in the Norman south door. The mediaeval village stood north of the church but has long since disappeared.

Following very good tracks across arable land past Tixover and Kilthorpe Granges we came to Ketton, a charming village where stone buildings were much in evidence. This area is famous for its stone quarries – at Ketton, Barnack and Collyweston. St Mary's church is a fine building, the third largest in Rutland. The great tower and stone spire date from 1300 and the west front, the oldest part, is transitional (c.1190). In the north wall of the chancel is a Victorian glass window dedicated to St Thomas Aquinas with the symbol of the Trinity above it.

We took a path by the river and then the main road into Tinwell whose church has a saddle-back tower of the 13th century and a chancel arch of same date. As time was running out we continued along the main road to Stamford where we visited St Martin's church which is principally of the Perpendicular period. We had time for our traditional "ceremonial tea" before making for the station to catch the train for Peterborough and London.

So we had completed our little round of Rutland and returned after five days of unbroken walking to our starting point. On all previous walks except that in the Isle of Wight (the second smallest county) we had finished at a different place from our starting point having usually followed some well-defined feature such as a ridgeway or river valley. But on this occasion we explored a fairly small area in depth – sometimes to the depth of a foot!

Tixover Church

Stone House at Ketton.

Ketton Church

The End of Iter XXVII

St Martin's Ch: Stamford

OAKHAM
All Saints

EDITH
WESTON
St MARY

TICKENCOTE
St PETER

EGLETON
St Edmund

BROOKE
St Peter

BRAUNSTON
All Saints

BELTON
St Peter

WARDLEY
St Botolph

DON'T
FLOOD
RUTLAND

RUTLAND·

MULTUM·IN·PARVO

A Scale of Miles
1   2

HANDS
OFF
RUTLAND

Tyghe

Ashwell   Market Overton

Whissendine   Barrow

Langham   Cotesmore

VALE   Burleythorp   Alesthorp
of   Burley   onth

o Flitteris   OKEHAM
SOKE   OKEHAM

Catmose

Braunston   the   Egleton   Hamb
Priory
LeeLodge   L
Brooke   Hamb
The Old
Maltins
Forest   thorp
Mainton
Belton   HUNDRED
Ridlington
of   Preston   Wing

Alston

Glaiston

Uppingham   Bisbrook

Wardley

Beamont   Liefield

Stokedry   Mor
Lyddington
Snelston   Seyton

Thorp

Caldecot   HUNDRED
Paro

Weland flu:

UPPINGHAM
St PETER
and PAUL

STOKE
DRY
St Andrew

LIDDINGTON
St Andrew

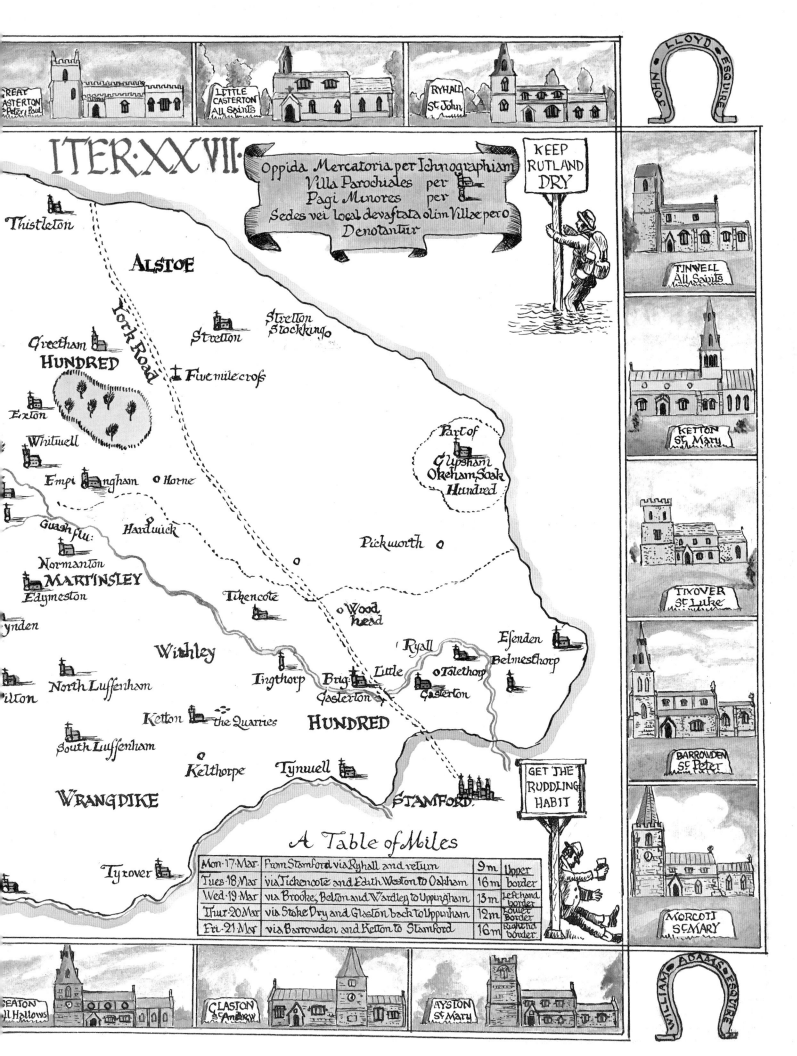

Arms of
WEST SUSSEX

REGNI
cui

Inn

COCKING

Linch
Down

813

South Downs

Way

A286

Heyshott
Down

South

Downs

Westdean Wood

Chilgrove

B2141

Long Barrow

Bow
Hill
670

Kingley
Vale

Stoke
Down

Wooden

East
Ashling

Inn

B2178

Earthwork

A27

Holt
Roman
Villa

FISHBOURNE

Cocking Church

UpWaltham Church.

Boxgrove Priory Church

The
Arms of
CHICHESTER

A285

Halnaker

Boxgrove

A27

Westhampnett

Hic Episcopus

The Fishbourne   Sea Horse

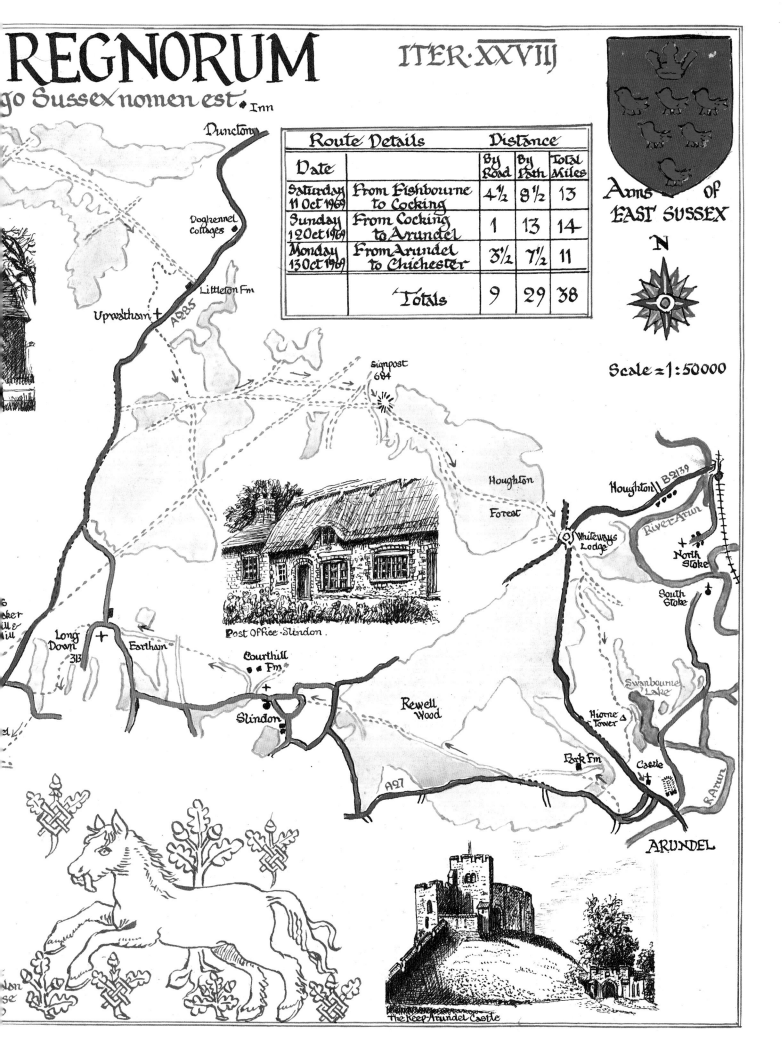

REGNORUM

...go Sussex nomen est. Inn

ITER·XXVIIJ

Arms of EAST SUSSEX

N

Scale = 1:50000

Route Details		By Road	By Path	Total Miles
Date				
Saturday 11 Oct 1969	From Fishbourne to Cocking	4½	8½	13
Sunday 12 Oct 1969	From Cocking to Arundel	1	13	14
Monday 13 Oct 1969	From Arundel to Chichester	3½	7½	11
	Totals	9	29	38

Duncton

Doghennel Cottages

Littleton Fm

Upwaltham

A285

Signpost 684

Houghton Forest

Houghton B2139

River Arun

North Stoke

South Stoke

Whiteways Lodge

Swanbourne Lake

Long Down 313

Eartham

Courthill Fm

Slindon

Rewell Wood

Hiorne Tower

Park Fm

Castle

R Arun

ARUNDEL

Post Office · Slindon.

A27

The Keep · Arundel Castle

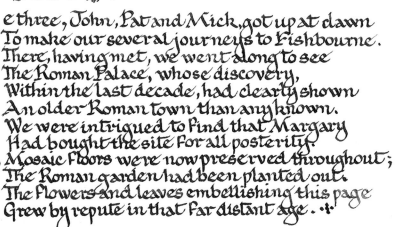

e three, John, Pat and Mick, got up at dawn
To make our several journeys to Fishbourne.
There, having met, we went along to see
The Roman Palace, whose discovery,
Within the last decade, had clearly shown
An older Roman town than any known.
We were intrigued to find that Margary
Had bought the site for all posterity.
Mosaic floors were now preserved throughout;
The Roman garden had been planted out.
The flowers and leaves embellishing this page
Grew by repute in that far distant age. ·:·

e left Fishbourne at nearly half past twelve,
No more time could be spared to 'dig and delve',
Then north we went and found, within a wood,
An old earthwork. There seemed some likelyhood
'Twas thrown up by the Atrebates tribe.
According to the Fishbourne Palace guide
They'd fled their capital at Silchester
To settle in the Selsey area,
Preferring rule by Roman to their king.
Within an hour we came to East Ashling;
Here in the Horse and Groom we had our fill
And so prepared to climb the nearest hill. ·:·

hence up Stoke Down the climb began until
Through clearing mist we saw ahead Bow Hill,
A noble spur which thrusts into the plains.
Here Britons fought a battle with the Danes;
Down there in Kingley Vale the trees of yew
Are said to number all the Danes they slew.
We climbed Bow Hill by long incline or "band";
As such a spur is called in Westmorland;
Where one may see Bow Fell, four times as high
Attracting walkers reaching for the sky.
Unlike that Fell, Bow Hill was clad with trees;
We sat down on the top and took our ease. ·:·

e had a parcel sent via Pat from Bill
Who'd asked him not to open it until
The first break for a smoke. We found within
A wrapper marked "Long Tom" around a tin
Of that most soothing weed, alleged by John
From certain ancient customs handed on.
In other words this fine tobacco ripe,
Perchance had fallen from the Queen's own pipe!
We took another break before Chilgrove;
We set up on a cart a tiny stove,
Put on the kettle and sat down with glee
To drink our first alfresco cup of tea.

ong Tom and tea, when taken after meals,
Should have propelled us easily one feels.
To Didling and to Bepton 'neath the Downs.
However, coming darkness gave us grounds
To choose the most direct route that we could,
And so we plunged straight into Westdean Wood.
We walked beneath a grove of tall larch trees
Along a grassy path up two valleys
Where Linchball Wood once stood, now in its stead
Were whin and willowherb all gold and red.
From this dense cover sprang a brace of deer;
They bounded off ahead to disappear.

he pathway ended 'neath the Down called 'Linch',
To reach it we were fighting every inch.
We broke the bramble tendrils with our sticks
And then backed up the slope – such sore tactics,
And bloody too, "but not a bloody race!"
Thought Pat as he dropped back to second place.
Upon the ridge we took the South Downs Way,
A new long distance path. One could not stray
From that clear path by day nor yet by night –
The chalk below worn turf showed up off-white.
We found the Richard Cobden Inn in Cocking
As good as any place we'd known to stop in.

ext morning we climbed up to Heyshott Down
Which loomed through mist above the little town.
While we were resting by a five-barred gate
There passed some sponsored walkers in full spate,
Their aim – to save the Wisborough Green church roof;
Its Horsham slabs were scarcely weather-proof.
The younger ones each vaulted o'er the gate,
Which shuddered violently beneath their weight.
And then the lovers, hand in hand they came,
Then older folk and one or two quite lame.
In order of agility and age
Man's several ages passed across the stage.

hen we arose they'd all gone out of sight
Save for the older ones who took delight
In all they saw; for them it was no race.
They'd get to Washington at their own pace.
As we came up they passed the time of day
Or chatted with us till we left the Way
To cross the flinty fields southward to search
For Upwaltham; its tiny Norman church,
Aisless and apsidal, standing alone,
Attracted us like some distant lodestone.
So strong its pull, we turned from Duncton Inn
And lunch-time found us therefore picnicking.

rom open pasture full of Southdown sheep
Our way led into woods both dense and deep.
Each track was marked with splendid new oak post
Inscribed "Footpath" or "bridlepath" at most
Six figure references would better show
Both where we were and where the path should go.
To find a route in that persistent mist
On nameless paths, our compass did assist.
Beyond West Wood, domain of noble beech,
We seemed to be on a familiar reach,
And realised 'twas Stane Street that we crossed.
We were quite pleased to find we were not lost.

o compensate for signposts with no name
We found one which put all of them to shame:
This way "to Bignor and Londinium"
It read, and this "to Slindon and Regnum".
Our way however lay to none of these,
But Houghton Forest and its varied trees.
"Through these delightful pathways we advanced",
While clearance of the mist the view enhanced.
Among pinewoods beside the track we found
Trees newly felled and scattered on the ground.
We sat down there and then to brew up char,
Not half a mile from a mobile tea bar.

wo miles remained to walk across the park
To Arundel as it was not yet dark:
Near Whiteways Lodge we passed a stand of beech,
Beyond which lay a secret, lovely reach,
A winding valley full of "Travellers' Joy",
The sort of place one dreamed of as a boy.
By Swanbourne Lake where herds of cattle lowed,
We left the vale, passed Hiorne Tower and strode
To Arundel, with evening mass in mind.
"If one would spend a day far from mankind",
Said E V Lucas, "there's no better way" –
Than that by which we three had walked this day.

eanwhile John toured the town and found an inn
Where ramblers had stayed that same weekend;
With two of them we passed the evening talking
About our rules and practices of walking.
Thus, we said that we always chose to wear
The clothes of a countryman to stand and stare
We must have time; and to another place
We'd travel rather than return to base;
Our party would not number more than four,
Whereas they liked to go with many more.
The difference that emerged from all our talk –
They liked to ramble whereas we would walk.

here was a Fitzalan who sought a Bull
To found a priest's college in Arundel.
Its chapel, being granted by the Crown
Stayed Catholic with this family renowned.
Today the chapel and the church are still
Together joined though parted by a grille.
A brick wall put up by the fifteenth Duke
After a most unfortunate law-suit,
Which claimed the chapel for the Anglicans,
Has been removed – a breath of tolerance.
So here if it were needed is some proof
Of men of different faith beneath one roof.

een from the west the town rose up on high
Crowned by the church of St Philip Neri.
We walked through Rewell Wood by bridle road
To Slindon where Hilaire Belloc abode;
And he, recalling happy childhood days,
Has given Sussex much unstinted praise.
"Regni Regnorum" he has christened it,
Nor can we think of any name more fit.
But he loved best the country west of Arun;
All other land to him was bleak and barren.
His influence lives on in Slindon still;
His voice may yet be heard on Duncton Hill.

e could not call at Slindon House but learned
How in the past its owners never turned
Away from Catholic faith. Here may be seen
The chapel on which that strong faith was weaned;
Here mass was said in secret under pain
Of capture by the pursuivants. Again
There is no doubt that many faithful priests
Were harboured here till persecution ceased.
A church was built a hundred years ago,
The secret chapel's successor; and so
When home in Slindon, Belloc could express
His pleasure once more to be near the mass.

By Courthill Farm there ran a flinty track;
It was dry the grass had died through lack
Of moisture; thence by swelling downs we came
To Eartham where the landord, Shaw by name,
Recalled his Boxer dog, now dead we fear.
We'd photographed him with a glass of beer
When he jumped up beside us on the seat,
Eight years ago when we explored Stane Street.
Then over Long Down where, beside our path,
The pheasants now enjoyed a fine dust bath.
Our route to Boxgrove though was somewhat baulked
By gravel pits round which we had to walk.

When Boxgrove Priory gave up its seal,
Lord de la Warr made eloquent appeal
For his "power chappell to be buried yn",
Which was refused. He bought it from the King,
And thus no doubt the Priory Church was saved,
The quire, the tower and the transepts, but the nave
Has gone, cloister and chapter-house as well;
The questen-hall stands in a field, a shell.
The transepts and the Early English quire,
Both vaulted splendidly, are much admired.
The painted floral Flemish decoration
Is reproduced in our illumination.

Rick had to leave for home, regrettably,
While Pat and John went on and brewed some tea;
We looked at Roman tiles at Westhampnett,
Then gave up walking at a roundabout,
Not seeking for a lift as several were;
We waited for a bus to Chichester.
Through Canon's Lane and Vicar's Close 'ere long,
We got there just in time for evensong.
We sat entranced before the great stone screen
As mens' and boys' voices sounded a paean
Of chants and hymns of praise so heavenly,
Our hearts and minds were raised spontaneously.

❖ The End of Iter XXVIII ❖

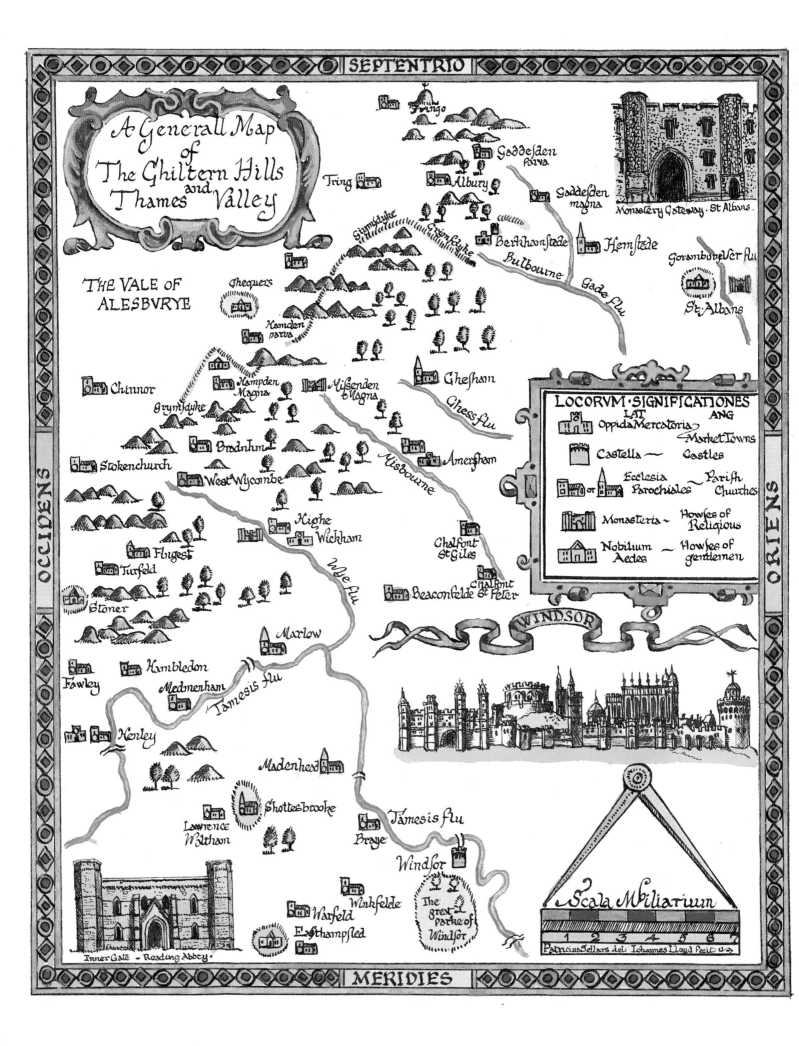

A Generall Map of The Chiltern Hills and Thames Valley

SEPTENTRIO

OCCIDENS

ORIENS

MERIDIES

THE VALE OF ALESBVRYE

Monastery Gateway. St Albans.

Tringe

Tring

Gaddesden parva

Albury

Gaddesden magna

Grymfdyke

Grymfdyke

Berkhamstede

Hemstede

Bulbourne

Gade flu.

Gorambury Vet flu

St. Albans

Chequers

Hamden parva

Chinnor

Hampden Magna

Grymfdyke

Missenden le Magna

Chesham

Chess flu.

Bradnhm

Amersham

Misbourne

Stokenchurch

West Wycombe

Highe Wickham

Flingest

Turfeld

Chalfont St Giles

Stoner

Beaconsfelde St Peter

Marlow

Hambledon

Wye flu.

Fawley

Medmenham

Tamesis flu.

Henley

Madenhead

Tamesis flu

Shottesbrooke

Braye

Lawrence Waltham

Windsor

Winkfelde

The great parke of Windsor

Warfeld

Easthampsted

Inner Gate – Reading Abbey.

WINDSOR

LOCORVM · SIGNIFICATIONES

LAT   ANG

Oppida Mercatoria   Market Towns

Castella   Castles

Ecclesia Parochiales   Parish Churches

Monasteria   Howses of Religious

Nobilium Aedes   Howses of gentlemen

Scala Miliarium

1 2 3 4 5 6 7

Patricius Sellars del: Iohannes Lloyd fecit:

Every area of chalk downland has its own character. The Chilterns are famed for their beech woods where one may walk unhampered by undergrowth beneath a canopy of delicate green. It is hard to say why we neglected so lovely an area in the past. Probably the proximity of London and its commuter belt discouraged us. It is true there are patches of built-up land in those valleys which point south-east towards London so allowing easy road and rail access. But centuries of under-population have left many empty quarters between these main arteries. They are jealously protected by the commuters themselves; and the Chilterns Society cares for the footpaths many of which are very beautiful and varied.

As Wordsworth, the connoiseur of scenery, would have done, we entered the Chilterns from the lowest side, the Thames valley; we then walked roughly on the lines of Grims Ditch across the valleys to Ivinghoe Beacon. On the last day we turned south east along a Roman road to Verulamium. The churches we saw are the subject of a separate contribution by Mick as the verses do not adequately describe them. Our route on the first four days was also a reconnaissance for a pony trek. This explains why Pat sometimes refused fences and went off alone along bridle paths. Also at the youth hostels he seemed more interested in finding stabling and hay than bed and breakfast. In the event the combined excercise showed that walkers have considerable advantages over riders in the matter of choice of paths. As to our earlier fears about the influence of London, traffic towns and residential areas were skirted or avoided although we were nearly always within thirty miles of The Great Wen.

The Old Roads of Coulsdon: Iter XXXI

Sunday 3rd January 1971

John was a member of a fifty-year-old rambling club called the Norbury Outpost. Pat and Mick joined them on a damp and misty January day because it was an area in which they had lived between the wars. So it was difficult to stifle the whiffs of nostalgia which kept bubbling up. The walk was ably led by Fred Rice, a sprightly sixty-six year old. There were also Owen Jones, Eddie Reiman, and Mick Tidy; Laurie Christy and John's son Robert aged eleven. We started from Coulsdon North station and soon came to the top of an old chalk-pit by a housing estate, children being protected from falling over the edge by an iron fence that would have kept lions in. Avoiding the houses we walked through a spinney where Laurie, who was an entomologist, talked about the wealth of insect life in ancient trees.

Beyond Cearn Way, which was still a flinty unmade road, we came to Coulsdon Court Golf Course and made a half circuit of its eastern perimeter – probably eight or nine holes. We took care to avoid the Sunday morning golfers who seemed to be everywhere driving off from fibre platforms on to temporary greens to reduce winter wear and tear of the course. The balls rose into the air or scudded into thickets perhaps to disappear from sight forever. John likened the whole weird scene to a Roman "ballistae" operation employing catapults called Onagers: named after a wild ass which kicks up stones with its hind hooves when pursued.

We arrived at length at Grange Park without being struck by a golf ball, or by a golfer for that matter; there we turned down Canons Hill to the valley bottom through which ran Caterham Drive. People looked up from their car-cleaning rituals to stare at the unusual sight of a number of men out walking for pleasure. As soon as possible we left them for a steep path up to Old Lodge Lane where we found the Wattenden Arms welcoming us all except poor Robert who was obliged to cool his heels in the porch. What a barbarous law it is that prevents children from entering such houses of warmth and refreshment on a winter's day. Fred had timed our arrival well for there were two spare tables.

We emerged somewhat later than intended to pass through the rest of the settlement known as Waddington. The name Wattenden Arms helps to preserve the name of the Domesday village of Watendone, derelict since the Middle Ages. We turned away from Kenley airfield to go down Waterhouse Lane. Rain was threatening but Fred seemed imperturbed by his lack of a coat; he said he had long ago shed all non-essential gear.

After recrossing the valley containing Caterham Drive we came upon Coulsdon Common which was instantly recognisable, beautifully unkempt and apparently unchanged in the past forty years. Near the Fox Inn there was a footpath sign to Happy Valley and Chaldon church. Down in the valley nothing stirred. It was splendid "greenbelt" country with occasional woods and flowing untrimmed hedges, all happily unspoiled. Our pace slowed perceptibly, the better to enjoy the scene. We came via the wood and a level meadow to the Chaldon Lane directly opposite Netherne hospital which was the first building we had seen since the Fox Inn.

Turning now towards Coulsdon we stopped by Devils Den Wood, now clear of undergrowth and full of handsome tall trees, to examine an iron post bearing the City of London Arms and the inscription 24, 25 Vict cap 42. We discovered later that it was a so-called "Coal Post" and one of many on the boundary of the Metropolitan Police area of London. They were authorised by an Act of Parliament in 1861 which extended the ancient Rights of the City of London for levying duties on all coal and wine coming into the City. The act was repealed in 1890 but the Coal Posts with their inscriptions referring to the statute still remain.

Ditches Lane from Chaldon used to end at the Wellcome Tea Rooms on Farthing Downs. We were dismayed to find it had been extended by a new road over the Downs to Coulsdon. Not unnaturally there had been fierce opposition from local conservationists, but a claim that the way across the Downs had always been a public highway carried the day. Truly one should never return to the scenes of one's boyhood. Studiously avoiding the new road we passed on by the two lone beech trees and the site of a Saxon cemetery, the burial place of Cuthraed from whom the name Coulsdon is derived. Mick was proud to have assisted Dr Brian Hope-Taylor in the excavation of the site.

At length and at dusk we came to the end of the Downs. Wild woodbine trailed across the hedgerows. We recalled how years ago we would break it in to short lengths to smoke it – at a time when schoolboys rarely used cigarettes. Our particular brand was not 'Woodbine' but 'Whiffy' and that was the final whiff of nostalgia before we returned to Coulsdon North station, which for a time bore the name of Coulsdon's first station, namely Stoats Nest.

But our recollections of less than forty years ago were as nothing compared with those we go on to relate of the history of the Old Roads of Coulsdon.

THE·NORBURY·OUTPOST· RAMBLING·CLUB·

The somewhat military ring to the name of the Club was intentional. In fact so keen were those old members to recall how and when they first met that an application was made, and special permission granted to include in the Club's badge the coat of arms of the Queen's Regiment. The badges were made of gun metal and were worn in lapels. As none has been issued since the original casting they are now rare.

The Club had its origin in the First World War. In those days local defence volunteers were recruited. When they were disbanded after the cessation of hostilities the members of the Norbury (London SW) unit missed the comradeship they had enjoyed. In an endeavour to capture some of the old spirit, various social activities were arranged such as dances and whist drives. Eventually it was decided to form an all male rambling club. This proved successful such that ever since, on the first Sunday of each month walks have been arranged except during the second World War when they were suspended.

None of those who first walked with the Club over fifty years ago are now with us. The present membership consists of a son and friends of the original members and friends of friends. Each month a different member volunteers to lead a walk. The route and timing are left entirely to his discretion. A Dinner is held annually followed by a Meeting where Club matters are discussed and the programme of walks for the next twelve months is arranged.

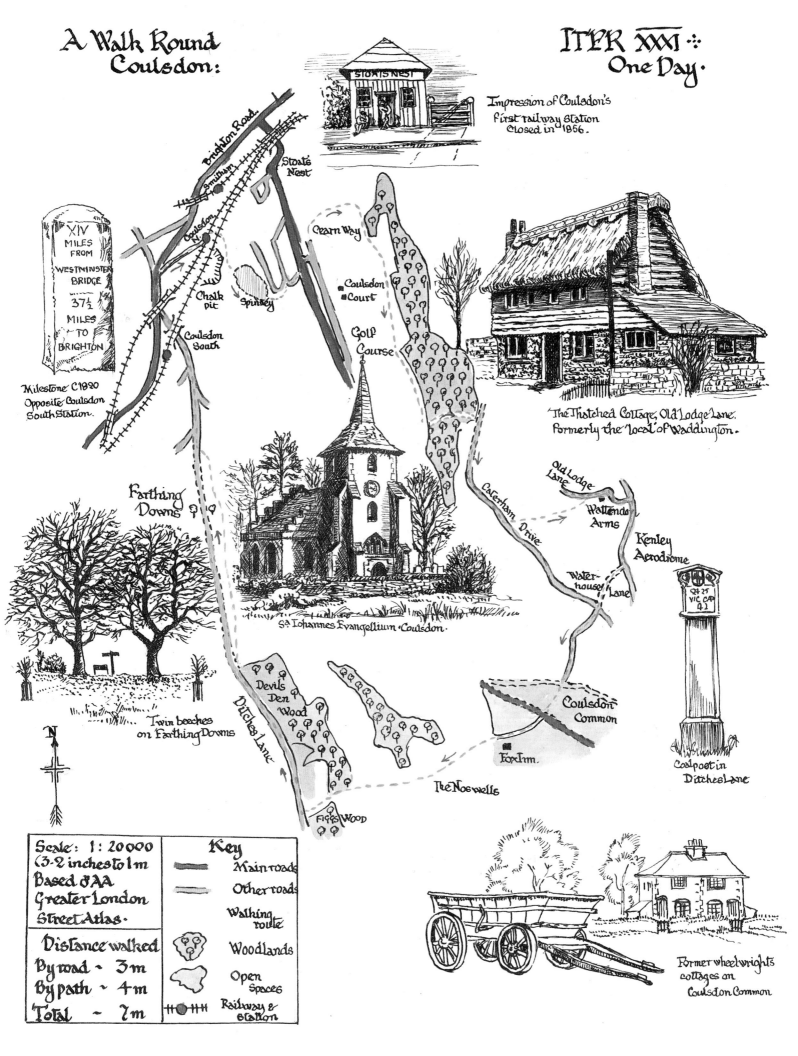

A Walk Round Coulsdon:

ITER XXXI ∴ One Day.

STOATS NEST

Impression of Coulsdon's first railway station closed in 1856.

Brighton Road

Smitham

Stoat's Nest

XIV MILES FROM WESTMINSTER BRIDGE 37½ MILES TO BRIGHTON

Milestone C.1820 Opposite Coulsdon South Station.

Coulsdon N.

Chalk Pit

Spinney

Coulsdon South

Cearn Way

Coulsdon Court

Golf Course

The Thatched Cottage, Old Lodge Lane. Formerly the 'local' of Waddington.

Old Lodge Lane

Wattendon Arms

Kenley Aerodrome

Caterham Drive

Water-house Lane

Farthing Downs

St. Iohannes Evangelium · Coulsdon.

Twin beaches on Farthing Downs

N

Devils Den Wood

Ditches Lane

Figgs Wood

The Noswells

Fox Inn

Coulsdon Common

84.25 VIC CAP 47

Coalpost in Ditches Lane.

Scale: 1:20 000 (3·2 inches to 1 m Based on AA Greater London Street Atlas.

Distance walked
By road ~ 3 m
By path ~ 4 m
Total ~ 7 m

Key
——— Main roads
——— Other roads
Walking route
Woodlands
Open spaces
Railway & station

Former wheelwrights cottages on Coulsdon Common

A perambulation of the fourteenth century compiled by the monks of Chertsey Abbey, then lords of the manor, defines the bounds of the manor of Colesdone. Beginning at Purleestrete (now Purley Oaks) and proceeding clockwise for twelve miles, first by Riddlesdown, it crosses the Godstone Road valley, turns west towards the Merstham Gap and Reigate road "and so by that highway as far as the cross in Smethedene, and so in Smethedene by the king's highway that leads towards Croydone as far as Purleystrete aforesaid".

The cross in Smethedene was the Leaden cross marked on John Seller's Map of Surrey in 1680. It was at the Road junction near the Red Lion, Coulsdon where the three parishes of Coulsdon, Woodmansterne and Beddington meet. Like the earlier perambulation, this map routes the road to Reigate past Portnalls and Chipstead leaving the future Brighton road blank. Smitham Bottom, a corruption of Smethedene ~"smooth valley"~ is shown unfenced throughout and is designated "Horse Race", a reminder of the growth of horse racing under Charles the Second.

John Aubrey wrote of Coulsdon in 1673, "In this parish lies Smitham Bottom, a place wherein Hazels flourish very much; here was formerly a Mercury or directory-post for Travellers, with Hands pointing to each Road ......". This may well have been the cross in Smethedene already referred to.

From the late eighteenth century the main road pattern remained much the same for over a hundred years. Marlpit Lane and Coulsdon Road fanned out from Bradmore Green while Old Lodge Lane and Hayes Lane did likewise from the hamlet of Waddington which had replaced the "lost village" of Watendone.

In 1850 Squire Thomas Byron built Coulsdon Court, now the Golf clubhouse, as his family seat. Then he stopped up the road which led from the Croydon - Reigate turnpike ~ Hartley Old Road ~ and made a new road ~ Hartley Down ~ on condition that the disused portion of the old road be handed over to him. Thenceforth Hartley Old Road led only to the Byron parkland and was barred by a gate.

Till 1856 there was no direct road from Coulsdon to Caterham. Previously the route lay along the western edge of Coulsdon Common and by Green Lane behind the present barracks. When a new more direct road over Coulsdon Common was made in 1856 the Old Fox and Sisters Pond were isolated.

In early times there were many driftways or farm-tracks. Many are now metalled roads but there remains one probably in its original form, a flinty bridleway between overgrown hedges. It runs from Woodplace Farm over Fairdene Down, now Farthing downs. It is still known locally as the Drift Lane.

This road crosses the earliest known road in Coulsdon which runs the length of Farthing downs. It may still be seen between hedge-row trees along the eastern boundary where ploughmen were foiled by the steepness of the slope. A later track followed the straight line along the summit. It was probably a track between Celtic fields about 100 a.d. and continued to be used by the Saxons who sited their burial mounds along its edges. Until after the last war, when it was reluctantly metalled, this ancient road remained in something like its mediaeval state, the whole surface of the Farthing downs being scored with alternative tracks over the turf.

EXMOOR is a region of such beauty and distinction that it was designated a National Park in 1954. Within its 250 odd square miles there is a wide variety of scenery. Its northern boundary is part of the Devon and Somerset coast ~ some thirty miles of high hogsback cliffs deeply cleft by rivers as at Lynton. The southern boundary lies where the moor merges gently into farmland threaded by the rivers Barle and Exe. Between the coast and the coast and the southern boundary lie the high moor and the Brendon Hills. Little moorland remains in the Brendons which are both farmed and afforested. But in the west, from Dunkery to the Chains, is a large area of moorland, heather and rough grass rising to several summits over fifteen hundred feet.

Exmoor is famous too for its ponies and wild deer. The true Exmoor pony is believed to be a genuine wild species. So also, and with more certainty is the Red Deer. They number at least five hundred and are the finest herds in England. Despite the damage they do to crops they are tolerated by the farmers who widely support the Devon and Somerset Staghounds. Pace, the anti-blood sports fraternity, the Red Deer probably owe their survival to the protection they thus enjoy.

In ancient times a Royal Forest, used for hunting and pasturing of ponies and sheep, lay around Simonsbath and was zealously preserved. But the Royal influence ended in 1818 with the sale of the land to John Knight, an energetic and wealthy iron-master from the Midlands. Throughout the rest of the century the Knights, father and son, managed this unpromising land. They broke up moorland, encouraged farm workers to live in the area and built roads and even built a wall around the estate.

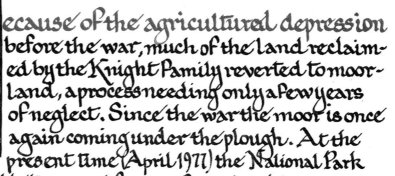

Because of the agricultural depression before the war, much of the land reclaimed by the Knight family reverted to moorland, a process needing only a few years of neglect. Since the war the moor is once again coming under the plough. At the present time (April 1977) the National Park Committee is unable to prevent farmers from ploughing moorland nor can it persuade them not to. Thus a farmer may refuse an offer of compensation for not ploughing because he thinks it inadequate and because he will be paid a grant by the Ministry of Agriculture if he ploughs. To try to resolve such conflicting legislation, the two departments concerned are to conduct an independent study of land use on Exmoor. Their aim should be to be to define an area of inviolate moorland and acquire it for the nation. The area would probably include most of the old Royal Forest.

Thus has the creation of a National Park sharpened the conflict between the interests of farmers and visitors. Conservative bodies like the Exmoor Society say that the moor should be ploughed no further. Although only a quarter of the National Park area is covered by moor, there may have been less in the nineteenth century. The intensity of moorland farming ebbs and flows. Exmoor's charms lies not so much in its moorland as in the colourful mix of moor and pasture.

In 1971 we returned to Exmoor for the first time since 1955. (Iter III · Volume I). So that we could enjoy the most varied pattern of moor and pasture and see more villages (albeit via steeper slopes) we encircled the moor instead of crossing it. Thus we followed very roughly the National Park boundary including much of the eastern coastal boundary. Steps were retraced in reverse from Porlock to Dunster and Winsford was revisited. We returned to our starting point at S.Molton after a fine five day walk.

EXMOOR:

The Way Ahead

Steam Roller near Brayford.
Working

The Former 'Ring O' Bells'

Saturday 20th March 1971

John, Pat, Mick and Bill set out from Blackwater, Surrey travelling in Bill's car. After passing by Stonehenge and noting excellent strip lynchets on Wiltshire hillsides we stopped at Mere whose church we had previously visited in 1962. Our next call was Glastonbury which we described in Volume I – Iter III. To that account we would add the sight of the Holy Thorn which was in full leaf and carrying remains of flowers; it blooms twice a year, at Christmas and in May.

Towards evening we reached South Molton and were made welcome by Mr and Mrs Ellarby. Jack, who was John's former colleague, had retired to this beautiful spot on the southern side of Exmoor. After supper we enjoyed watching the Calcutta Cup match on colour television – a rare treat for some of us at that time.

From South Molton to Lynton
Sunday 21st March 1971

It was Mothering Sunday; Mrs Ellarby went to a service at the parish church where the children would present wild daffodils to their mothers. Jack kindly took us in his car some seven miles to Brayford whence we began the ascent of Exmoor. A steep footpath brought us to All Saints, High Bray which has a very good south arcade c.1480 with traces of pigmentation. The original 15th-century rood screen stands across the tower arch. Then going northwards along delightful lanes we came across a steamroller which Mick photographed. A lane followed the boundary of the National Park at about one thousand feet above sea level. Near Four Cross Way we saw several tumuli, went on over Fullaford Down and so into Challacombe where we enjoyed a midday break at the Black Venus Inn, formerly the Ring O'Bells. The winds grew stronger as we ascended Challacombe Common. We reached our highest ever point (1450 feet) a little to the west of Chapman's Barrows where snow lay about in places. We did not see the standing stones but passed an inscribed stone in memory of "Robin". Across Parracombe Common there was a narrow lane with a hedge which kept the wind off. After a long descent we came to Martinhoe Cross where a letter-box bore the legend "Woody Bay Station" which was on the Lynton and Barnstaple Railway; this was closed as a line in 1935.

On Challacombe Common

We brewed up in a wooden bus shelter. Smoke poured from burning bus tickets which we used to supplement our fuel. We escaped from the wind eventually by going down a wooded ravine to Lee Bay, a splendid sight far below the tower on Duty Point. To the west beyond Crock Point we had a glimpse of Woody Bay and the high cliffs beyond it. We turned in the opposite direction past Lee Abbey and a Conservation Year exhibition of local natural features. Then we entered the wild and beautiful Valley of the Rocks encountering wild white goats on Castle Rock. We followed two of them along a precarious ledge carved from the seaward face of Hollerday Hill. The sea was calm and the flowering gorse was a picture in the evening light. Ascending to Lynton we tried three places before finding accommodation at the Neubian Guest House kept by James and Sylvia Peacock high on the hill in Lynton.

LEE BAY

From Lynton to Porlock
Monday 22nd March 1971

It was a glorious sunny day. We returned down the steep hill into Lynmouth and picked up the path by the East Lyn River which we followed for two hours to Rockford, sometimes beside and sometimes high above it. The fairly easy path led through delightful woods, mostly of oak with occasional clearings and deep gorges in the rock as at Myrtleberry Cleave. At Barton Wood men were planting hemlock.

A young labrador followed us from Rockford to Brendon where we lunched at the Stag Hunters Inn. Only one customer seemed to be a local. He wore a groom's leggings and sat in his corner seat. We left the river after another mile to make for the coastal path. This entailed a steep climb to County Gate on the Devon and Somerset border. Close by is a Roman fortlet, probably a Signal Station. We could see the earthworks. The long distance coastal footpath ran at least half a mile from the shore because of the nature of the so called "hogsback" cliffs which steepen towards the sea. It was an exhilarating walk under a clear blue sky and in complete contrast to the morning march up the East Lyn river bank.

A 'Local' at the Stag Hunters Inn.

Eventually the path made a steep descent to Culbone where a tiny church nestled in the woods close to a picturesque pottery. Culbone church is one of the smallest complete parish churches in England, the nave and chancel being only thirty-five feet in length overall. The nave roof, choir screen and some of the oak pews date from 15th century. There is a good Norman bowl font.

Culbone Church.

Culbone ~
Grotesque.

The "Ship Inn"

Porlock
Church

On the north wall of the chancel there was a two-light round-headed window cut from a single slab of sandstone – probably Saxon. There was a grotesque head carved on the mullion outside.

Somehow we lost the way-marked path beyond Culbone; instead we found a private road through Yearnor Wood into Worthy whence we looked across Porlock Bay to Selworthy Beacon. To avoid the road to Porlock we took a path at Porlockford. It had been badly cut up by horses' hooves.

At Porlock we booked in at the Ship where the poet Southey once stayed. It was an attractive inn with thatched roof and round white chimney typical of this area. We soon learned that the Devon and Somerset Staghounds had met that morning at the Ship; we drew our own conclusions about the state of the path at Porlockford.

From Porlock to Dunster   *Tuesday 23rd March 1971*

This was to be the easiest and shortest day so we took it easy, avoiding both Selworthy Beacon and the Grabbist which John and Val had taken in their stride in 1955. First we visited the church of St Dubricius which contains a fragment of a late Saxon cross and a very ancient 15th-century clock with stone weights. We then took pleasant lanes across the levels to Bossington and Lynch at the foot of Selworthy Beacon. Lynch chapel was formerly a manorial chapel restored to ecclesiastical use in 1885 after use as a barn since the Reformation. At Allerford we crossed the river by an ancient pack-horse bridge and took an old high-level track up to Selworthy, the famous show village of white walled thatched cottages. John alleged he had seen besmocked inhabitants sitting on stools outside their cottages smoking clay pipes and waiting to be photographed. The church cleaners were displeased with us even though we left our shoes in the porch as though entering a mosque. The most notable feature of this church is the beautiful wagon roof in the south aisle c.1538.

Our route continued by lanes well above the valley across which we looked at Dunkery Beacon, the highest point of Exmoor. Soon we came to Tivington where there is a manorial chapel like that of Lynch. For many years it was used as a dwelling and still has a thatched roof. By lanes again we reached Wootton Courtenay where we stopped at the Dunkery Hotel. The bar was closed for re-decoration but we were admitted to the billiard room where we sat on horsehair sofas.

Roof of South Aisle -1538
All Saints - Selworthy.

All Saints Church has a good holy-water stoup in the south porch and two pillar niches in the north arcade. The saddleback tower is unusual. We followed a lane down the Avill valley until Mick suddenly drew attention to a path on the left called Avill Way. It went up quite steeply and turned along the side of Knowle Hill but later we lost it at a combe. At length we picked up a private path in a forest and returned to the valley and Dunster by the lower slopes of Grabbist Hill.

There was time to visit the beautiful priory church of St George with its magnificent rood screen spanning nave and aisles. John and Val had admired it in the course of Iter III (recalled in Volume I). Unhappily the dovecote, which contains a revolving ladder for reaching the nests, was locked up. The dovecote was probably built by the Norman Baron de Mohun and was afterwards maintained and improved by the prior and six monks from Bath Abbey. We enjoyed a Devon cream tea near the Yarn Market. We had difficulty finding accommodation, trying five places. Off-season in a tourist area can indeed be difficult and we should have booked in advance. We lost no time in booking by telephone for the following night at Winsford, having found Earlham guest house in Dunster after so many rebuffs.

From Dunster to Winsford   *Wednesday 24th March 1971*

We set off by way of the old Gallox Bridge, an old pack-horse bridge and entered Dunster Park from which there were fine views. We called at the church of St John the Baptist at Carhampton which contains a glorious screen (reported in Iter III). To avoid the steep hill to the south we took the lane to Withycombe, an attractive village whose church of St Nicholas had escaped enlargement in the Perpendicular period. The rood screen is typical of the district and is believed to have been made at Dunster about 1500. The fine holy water stoup is, unusually, on the left-hand side of the porch.

We could no longer avoid the Brendon Hills and so climbed via Combe Farm to the highest point of Croydon Hill where, at 1,255 feet we took a well-earned rest in the bracken. A track led to Kingsbridge where we stopped at the Royal Oak for our midday meal break. The bar, supported by stone pillars was only large enough for one person at a time. From a valley containing a chain of small lakes we climbed again through Chargot Wood where a deer bounded away into the trees. On the main Brendon ridge we turned along the track of an old mineral railway to a disused iron mine at Gupworthy.

All Saints Church – Wootton Courtenay.

The Yarn Market – Dunster

Rood Screen – St Nicholas – Withycombe.

Winsford

Caratacus Stone and Shelter

Tarr Steps

Here in a shed by the mineshaft and an old chapel we brewed up tea. Gupworthy was a desolate deserted area. Even the sheep seemed so surprised to see us that they ran towards us. Maybe they thought we had food for them. Near Armoor it began to rain and we "caped up" for the first time in two years. Descending towards the Exe valley and calling briefly at the church in Exton, we were lucky to discover an old burial path which provided a short cut to the Winsford Road. Our planned meeting with Mr and Mrs Ellarby worked to perfection for they arrived at Winsford at the same time as ourselves. We entertained them to a splendid dinner of roast fowl and apple tart at Karslake Guest House. John and Val had stayed here in 1955; Mrs Jenkins cooked the meals on both occasions.

Winsford to South Molton — *Thursday 25th March 1971*

e set out to climb Winsford Hill by the route taken by John and Val in 1955. It was a hard climb to Spire Cross which was the same height as Croydon Hill. Near the top is the intriguing Caratacus stone, about four feet high with an inscription which reads CARAACI NEPVS or Kinsmen of Caratacus. The inscription is attributed to the Dark Ages but the stone could have been erected much earlier.

Beyond Winsford Hill we turned off to Knaplock with a view to walking by the River Barle to Tarr Steps where we paused for reflection. We could not tell the age of this great stone clapper bridge but we knew some of the stones had been shifted by flood waters and restored to their correct position at least twice in the past twenty years. As we went on by the river, John recalled seeing a man fishing there in 1955 in a minimum of water. He had remarked philosophically that the water was lower the year before.

There followed another steep climb up to Hawkridge Common. Much of the common had been ploughed up and enclosed, an example of the encroachment on the moor described in the preface. But the Dane's Brook valley, where we crossed back into Devon, was much more wild and interesting. We crossed the brook by an odd bridge, consisting of a fence-like structure suspended from a pole apparently intended to prevent cattle and sheep from straying. At Lyshwell on the slope beyond the farmer explained to us how he transferred lambs who'd lost their mother to a ewe who'd lost her lambs by placing over them the skins of the dead lambs; otherwise the ewe would not accept the lambs who were not her own.

Beyond Anstey Gate on the high southern ridge we turned along the National Park boundary for about a mile. The boundary hedgerow was littered with large coloured plastic bags intended, as we later discovered, to deter the deer from entering the farmland below the moor. It seemed a pity to spoil the scene with such unsightly litter. We saw a few wild ponies, but no deer. We finally left the moor at Smallacombe and went down to the London Inn at Molland. Here, where we ate and drank, was a collection of animals and birds comprising the London Inn Zoo. We heard about a tame deer called Ernest who used to drink beer in the bar. St Mary's church was worth a visit. The late Perpendicular arcade was two feet out of true and supported by lateral timbers. There were high box pews, a three-decker pulpit and stocks in the south porch. There was also a picture showing a stag at bay in the porch with the hounds outside; it was called 'Sanctuary'.

Hanging Fence across the Danes Brook

By lanes and tracks south-west from Molland we descended to the valley of the River Yeo and came to the disused station of Bishops Nympton and Molland on the Taunton to Barnstaple line which was closed in 1966. There is a plan to convert some twenty miles of this line to a greenway for recreational use but unhappily the stretch on which we now set out had already been sold. The ballast was still in situ so after about a mile we abandoned the route for what proved to be an even more difficult one through rough grass and water holes to a camp on a hill above Whitechapel Moors where we brewed up tea for the last time.

Rejoining the railway line at Rawstone Moors, we found the remaining mile and a half was much easier. Then from the former South Molton station a good asphalt footpath led up to the town. We reached Jack Ellarby's bungalow just as darkness was falling. Having enjoyed an excellent supper of sausages and mash we settled down to watch colour TV and later go for our usual drink.

Disused Station.

Friday 26th March 1971

We thanked Jack Ellarby and his wife for their hospitality and set out in Bill's car to cross the moor in fewer hours than we had taken days to walk it. We spent some time in Wells where we visited the parish church of St Cuthbert and, of course, the cathedral – described in Iter III. After lunch we made for Guildford where we enjoyed a "ceremonial" tea at a well-known cafe near the railway station. We reflected on the splendid walk. It had been hard going at times but the memories would be sweeter.

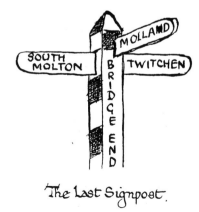

The Last Signpost.

The End of Iter XXXII

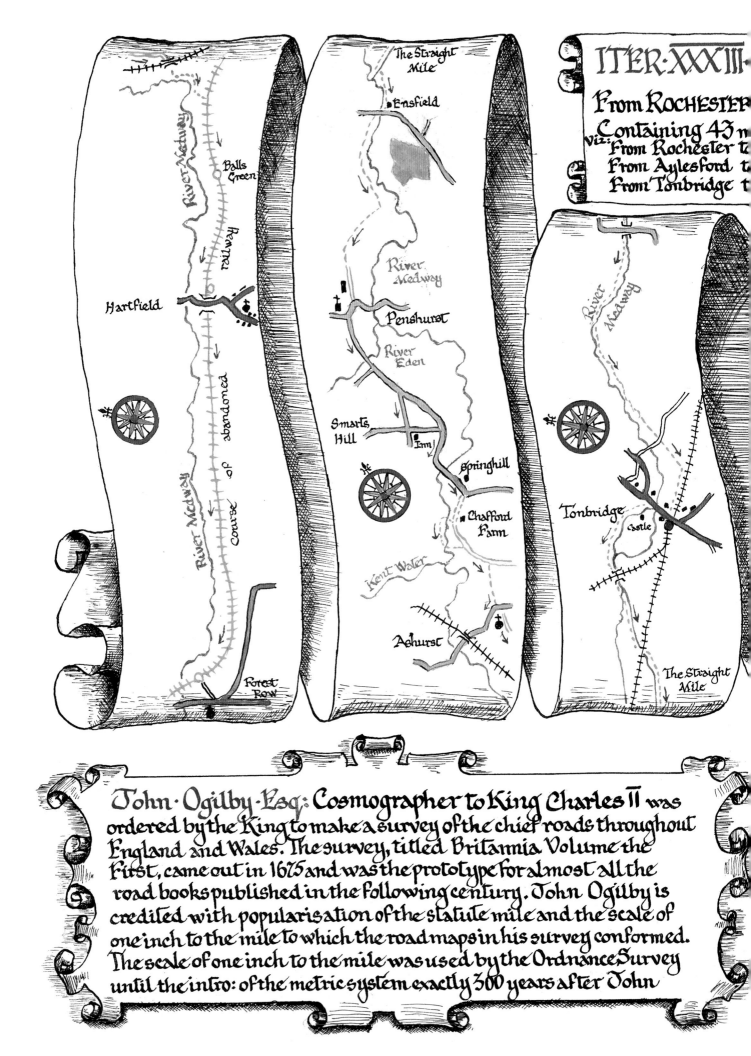

ITER XXXIII

From ROCHESTER

Containing 43 m[iles]
viz: From Rochester t[o]
From Aylesford t[o]
From Tonbridge t[o]

John·Ogilby·Esq: Cosmographer to King Charles II was ordered by the King to make a survey of the chief roads throughout England and Wales. The survey, titled Britannia Volume the First, came out in 1675 and was the prototype for almost all the road books published in the following century. John Ogilby is credited with popularisation of the statute mile and the scale of one inch to the mile to which the road maps in his survey conformed. The scale of one inch to the mile was used by the Ordnance Survey until the intro: of the metric system exactly 300 years after John

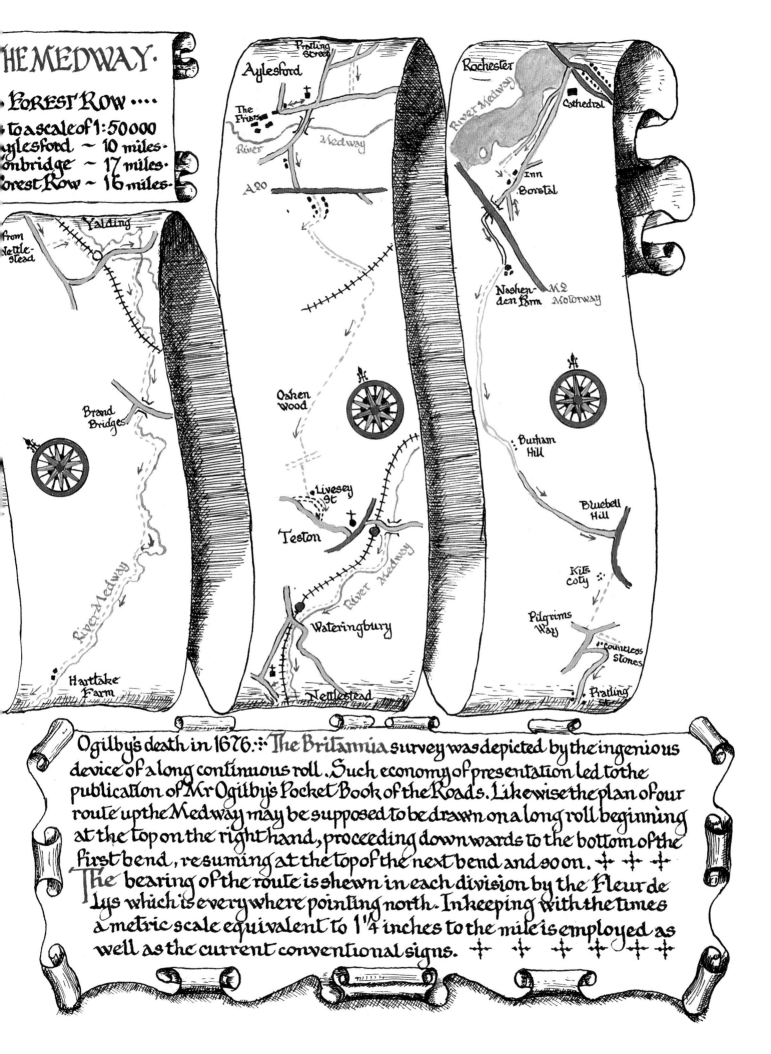

THE MEDWAY.

FOREST ROW ....

to a scale of 1:50000

Aylesford ~ 10 miles.
Tonbridge ~ 17 miles.
Forest Row ~ 16 miles.

Ogilby's death in 1676. ✛ The Britannia survey was depicted by the ingenious device of a long continuous roll. Such economy of presentation led to the publication of Mr Ogilby's Pocket Book of the Roads. Likewise the plan of our route up the Medway may be supposed to be drawn on a long roll beginning at the top on the right hand, proceeding downwards to the bottom of the first bend, resuming at the top of the next bend and so on. ✛ ✛ ✛ The bearing of the route is shewn in each division by the Fleur de lys which is everywhere pointing north. In keeping with the times a metric scale equivalent to 1¼ inches to the mile is employed as well as the current conventional signs. ✛ ✛ ✛ ✛

Of English inland counties, Shropshire is the largest but it remained unknown to us till now. We had long imagined it, remote and beautiful as described in Housman's poems "The Shropshire Lad" and in the novels of Mary Webb, the so-called "Shropshire Lass". We chose to walk among the hills south of the Severn and we were not disappointed. We had a strong sense of closeness to the Welsh mountains, there was great variety in the terrain and a certain uniqueness in the landscape.

We were amongst ancient rocks whose many formations in a small area make it a happy hunting ground for geologists. Our first hill was that outlier, the Wrekin, and then we crossed the Severn following more or less the line of the Church Stretton Fault – a great crack in the earth's crust. The oldest pre-Cambrian rocks lie beside this Fault. We climbed the height on the most of it, the Long Mynd, and returned over it the next day to go down to Ludlow. Thence we went into Corvedale, climbed the slopes of Brown Clee Hill and traversed the long limestone ridge of Wenlock Edge. Finally we re-crossed the Severn at Buildwas and returned to Wellington.

The map opposite is based upon Saxton's map of Shropshire. He called it Salopia, the Latin form of Salop in 1577. It seems the Normans prefferred Salopes cira (or Salop for short) to the original name which was Scrobbesbyrigscir. That was hardly surprising. However on 1 April 1980 the name Salop was dropped in favour of Shropshire, thus ending an unnecessary ambiguity in favour of a simple form of the original name. It was a better fate than that which overtook Rutland a few years ago.

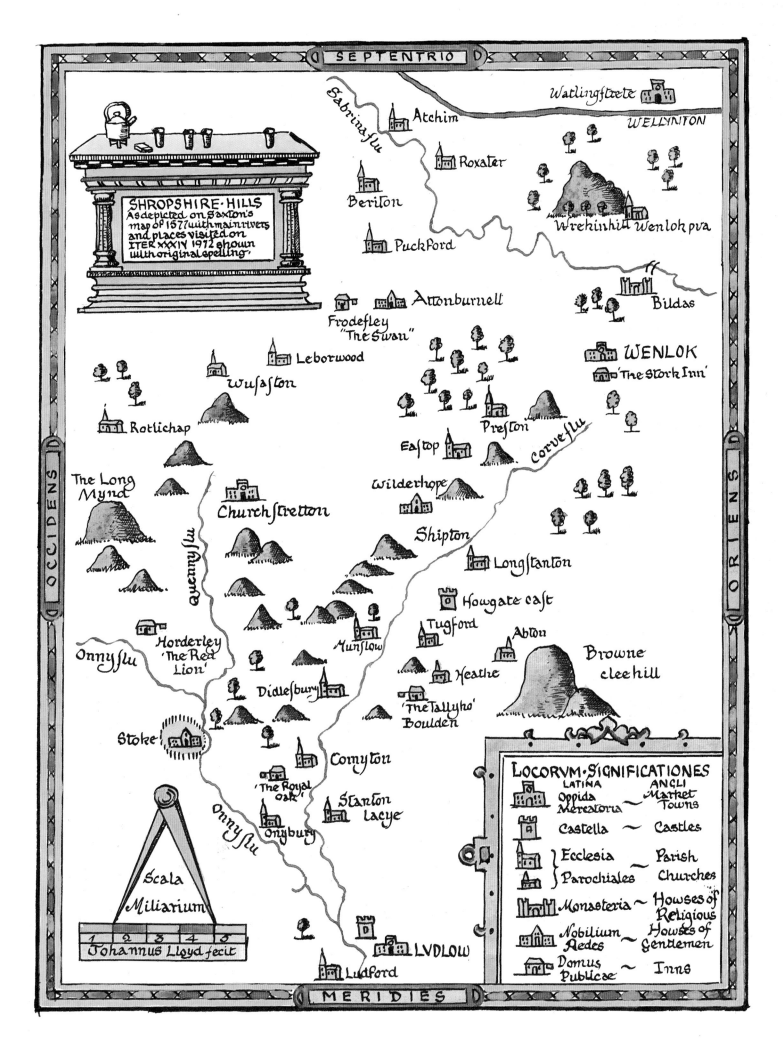

Our first walk along the Pilgrim's Way involved four of us. Since Val's untimely death in 1960 our numbers have been increased by newcomers whom we ought now to introduce. Sam Weller performs this task in the first person in the Prologue which follows this preface. He is field officer of the Billericay Archaeological and Historical Society. Through his good offices we were privileged to present our tales (with due apologies to Geoffrey Chaucer) to that Society in March 1977. It also seems appropriate to re-tell these tales here as the first walk in this Volume takes us once more to Canterbury.

We are all well met in Southwark, not at Chaucer's Tabard, but at the Harrow in Stoney Street. This was one of a number of inns where we were accustomed to meet over the years to sustain our friendship and plan forthcoming walks. Up to this time we had always met at a Southwark inn convenient to London Bridge Station, our earliest being the Kings Head in Southwark High Street. However, at the close of this Volume in 1978 we are at the Royal George in Carlisle Lane near Waterloo and from there we went north of the river to Henekey's in Trump Street in the City. There followed a few meetings in the Hogarth Room of the Ludgate Cellars, but at the time of writing we meet in the former crypt of the church of St Mary Magdalen near Regents Park. With stained glass windows about us, and a bar not too far away we are well set up to continue our plans, which include from 1974 onwards an annual dinner with our wives. The minutes are faithfully kept by Mick but the years cannot be thus neatly captured. One final word: the Viatores seems a fitting new name for the group. We must acknowledge its original employment by the colleagues of Ivan Margary when they wrote jointly a new book about Roman roads.

Omnes homines aequi in via sunt:

The New Canterbury Tales ~ Prologue ∴

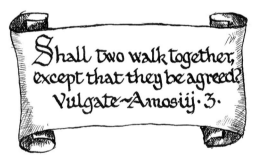

Shall two walk together, except that they be agreed? Vulgate ~ Amos iij · 3 ·

"And we only came in to see the Rood-screen."

The Viatores take things in their stride
When walking through the English countryside.
In Coronation year they set off merrily
To walk the Pilgrims Way to Canterbury
Though Valentine turned off the long green way
To walk a road that none may walk but he;
The others are still here: there's Mick the Ship,
Who joined them down in Kent on their first trip,
The Scribe, the Clerk; now Bill the Exciseman,
And latterly there's George, the Fisherman,
And Jack who knew them from an earlier day.
He was the one that never got away.
And there's another Bill who bound this book;
The dust from off his feet he's not yet shook.
And last of all but certainly not least
There's Father Smith who is a godly priest.
Oh, by the way, my name is on the list –
I'm their consultant archaeologist.

I met them as it happened in this way,
At Southwark at the Harrow Inn one day.
They were discussing plans for their next trip.
I was admitted to their fellowship.
I'll tell you shortly how they looked to me
According to profession and degree,
And what apparel they'd be walking in
So with the Scribe I will my tale begin.

With pen and ink-horn on a winter's day
In his scriptorium he works away
At fine calligraphy on every page,
Well worthy of the mediaeval age.
Each map and drawing he delineates
And prefaces and such illuminates.
In twenty years two thousand miles he's done.
That's many miles ahead of anyone.
He's never missed a walk; once hurt his knee
And missed some miles through tripping on a tree.
He wears a 'winkle shooter' on his head
But when it rains says he should have instead
A brick hat with down-pipe and soakaway.
The best thing that he ever made, they say

Is an elixir heated on a fire,
Which seems to satisfy their hearts' desire.
When he has fixed a place to exercise
His esoteric craft, he looks most wise.
Down in a windless corner he will squat
Until he has pronounced the water 'hot'.
The tea then made for every single man
Is numbered to accord with Ringelman;
And if that number seems to them too large
They add hot water and declare it 'sparged'.
Then each one raises up his plastic cup
To praise the brew – also to drink it up.

Now here's a London Clerk whose name is Pat.
He pores a great deal over maps and that.
He has a hollow look and sober wear;
The thread upon his jacket is quite bare
He's worn his old green hat since being 'demobbed';
He bought a new one once but he was robbed.
He also wears a pair of Home Guard gaiters.
He doesn't care too much about his status.
He plans the route to walk with utmost care
And then decides there isn't time to spare.
He'll say "Turn right through this great heap of dung!"
He cannot hope to have his praises sung.
He'll say "Be sure, we'll reach the inn at one",
And then at two, God's life, they're nearly done.
There's no time for a drink before it shuts.
He must think that they are a lot of nuts.
He used to stop to write notes by the way,
Or check his maps. It only caused delay;
And so for years this leader used to follow
Just like the famous Duke of Plaza Toro.
But now he takes a pocket tape-recorder.
You'd think there'd be a little less disorder;
But not at all, he still gets left behind.
However, I don't wish to be unkind.
He says they're never lost – its just that he
Is in a circle of uncertainty.
At least he's skilled enough at navigation
To make sure that they reach their destination.

His brother Mick, the Shipman, is fair game.
His boats ply under "Sealink". Mick says "Shame
On me!" They're ships; not boats. In British Rail
He earns his keep, not surely under sail.
Now as their walks start here and finish there,
He says which train to catch. As to the fare
He tells them they must dip into their pockets.
In consequence he gets a few mild rockets.
But when they have to cross a stile that's old
Then he is really worth his weight in gold:
They send him over first. Should it collapse,
Why then they've spared themselves a few mishaps!
Moreover, in the depths of his rucksack,
He seems to carry all the things they lack.
So when the wind blows cold some blanket pins
He'll find to fix their coats beneath their chins.
They've even known him fix a broken zip
With safety pins; he learned that on his ship.
And when it comes to scissors or to string,
Or sticking plaster, he's got everything.
However, what they cannot understand
Is why he takes a hair brush with him, and
I'm told that he is now the only one
Who puts on shorts should there be any sun.
He measures up the distance walked each day
Then gazing round the dim lit bar, he'll say
"How many miles today? Come have a try!"
And thinking with their feet they make reply.

The Exciseman I'll introduce the next.
His name is Bill – what else could you expect?
He knows the mysteries of V.A.T.
And also of specific gravity.
With well trained palate each new beer he'll savour.
He can distinguish Ruddles by the flavour.
Their own tobacco may cause him some trouble –
That Long Tom Country Mixture, rough as stubble.
He dare not confiscate it when it's ripe;
'Twould not be suited for the 'Queen's own pipe'.
She couldn't celebrate her Jubilee
With Long Tom in the stoves, most unseemly.

He joined the walkers some five years ago.
He's done five hundred miles – a splendid show!
But wait! He's worn the same red socks throughout.
He hasn't even turned them inside out.
He's very good at finding inns to stay;
He's better even than Egon Ronay.
He buys the butter and the bread and cheese
And always does his level best to please.
You will have gathered that the Exciseman
Belies his calling, is in fact a nice man,
Also he wears an elegant deerstalker,
And is a parfait gentlemanly walker.

Now George has quite an interesting line –
Coarse Fisherman. On Iter Thirty-nine
When rain came down all day, he didn't care,
He just likes being in the open air.
Next time they walked him twenty miles and more,
No wonder that his feet were very sore.
Half-way he had to buy some brand new shoes;
He'd not give up. What! Give up all that booze?
Coarse walking he did readily embrace
Despite the wettest walk on Cranborne Chase.
He dresses like the other vagabonds.
At any rate his clothing corresponds.
That's not surprising as their walking code
Is that "all men are equal on the road".
With his calligraphy they're satisfied
That he is very nearly qualified
To understudy John as a "subscriber",
Not only that, he is a fair imbiber.
And if you want to know how much, I reckon
He does some thirty miles to the gallon.

I ought to tell you there's an absentee,
A member of this confraternity.
He is their chaplain, Father Smith. I'm told
He stayed away to watch over his fold
That's why he cannot often walk with them
Nor come to London and the Harrow Inn.
In sickness or in grief he'll pay a call.

He is quite elderly and very tall;
He wears an overcoat of darkish shade
And rather long; and in his hand a stave
With handle carved. Also an Austrian hat
And at his throat sometimes a silk cravat.
And he has such a long and steady stride
It's not so easy to remain beside
Him on the road. He much enjoys a walk
And is also a learned man, a clerk
And rich in holy thoughts to say the least
We think there never was a better priest.

There is a Bookbinder, by name Bill Ward
He's bound these books for years without reward.
In handsome leather each quinquennium
He turns out yet another fine volume.
No doubt he has enjoyed the best of schooling
To make a Book of Walks with such good tooling.
Some pilgrim badges he has cast anew
From Walsingham and Canterbury too,
And these were worn in nineteen seventy eight
On his first walk – 'twas Iter Forty-eight.
When Bill then joined them on the dusty road
He helped sometimes to ease their heavy load,
For he is qualified to give First Aid
Thus aches and pains and blisters he allayed.

And there's an Egyptologist, Jack Coombs
Who spends some time investigating tombs.
He was the first who did receive report
On daily postcards plain of our first walk.
These were retained and so helped clerk and scribe
The Pilgrims Way adventure to describe.
Jack lives on Watling Street in Kent; I'll wage
He is best placed to start a pilgrimage.

I've told you all about the Viatores.
Let's go ahead and listen to their stories.
They're off to Canterbury – well, God speed!
Blessed St Thomas answer to their need!

✦ WALKERS' WISDEN ✦
LVSTRA · I~IV ~ 1953~73 · (Itinera I ~ XXXVI) ⁖

Total Mileages.	Total miles walked	Iter Nº		Miles 2037	Percents
	Total miles by path			1083	53·2%
	Personal mileages		John on 150 days	2037	100 %
			Pat on 139 days	1863	92 %
			Mick on 133 days	1773	87 %
			Bill on 41 days	561	28 %
			Cuthbert on 8 days	100	5%
Highest County Mileages.			Sussex 286: Wiltshire	165	
			Kent 204: Hampshire	141	
			Dorset 190: Surrey	117	
Annual Mileages & Weather.			Highest 1965~66 ~155m: av.	102	
	Wettest season		1967~8 with rain during	33	24 %
	Driest season		1956~7 with negligible rain	~	~
	Overall weather		1953~73 with rain during	212	10·4%
Iter Mileages.	Average iter mileage		for itinera I ~ XXXVI	56·5	
	Longest continuous itinera	XXXVI	Bath to Besselsleigh	107	
		XXXII	Brayford to South Molton	68	
	Most daily average miles	XX	Icknield Way	16·4	
		I	The Pilgrims Way	16	
	Most daily path miles	XX	Icknield Way	10	
		XXVIII	Regni Regnorvm	9·7	
	Highest proportion of paths	XXVIII	Regni Regnorum		76%
		XIII	London ~ Lewes Way		69%
Daily Mileages.	Average daily mileage		over 150 days	13·6	
	Most miles in a day	I	Kemsing to Hollingbourne	23	
		XX	Ashwell to Gt. Chesterford	21	
	Most path miles in a day	VIII	Salisbury to Tollard Roy:	15	
		XXVIII	Cocking to Arundel	13	
	Highest proportion of paths	XXVIII	Cocking to Arundel		93%
		XXIX	Lee Gate to Ivinghoe		83·5%
	Most miles before lunch	XVI	Fontmell Magna to Martin	13·8	
	Most miles after lunch	XX	Goring to Watlington	13	

Highest Points reached.				Longest itinera:	
	Mountains (over 1000')	Winsford Hill 1405	III	Icknield Way Iter XX	114·5
		The Long Mynd 1400	XXIV	Pilgrims Way Iter I	112
	Hills (under 1000')	Walbury Hill 975	VII	South Cotswolds Iter XXIV	108
		Long Knoll 944	XII	South Shropshire Iter XXIV	82

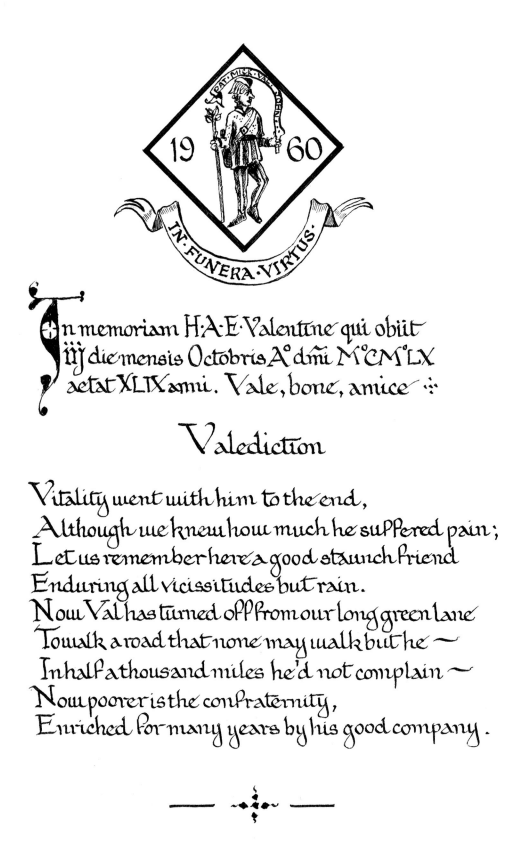

In memoriam H·A·E·Valentine qui obiit iiij die mensis Octobris A° dñi M°CM°LX aetat XLIX anni. Vale, bone, amice ⁖

Valediction

Vitality went with him to the end,
Although we knew how much he suffered pain;
Let us remember here a good staunch friend
Enduring all vicissitudes but rain.
Now Val has turned off from our long green lane
To walk a road that none may walk but he ~
In half a thousand miles he'd not complain ~
Now poorer is the confraternity,
Enriched for many years by his good company .

Authors' Note

'A BOOK OF WALKS'

THE ORIGINAL WORK is written in 'half uncial' or cursive script. Like modern lower case, this was derived from the Roman capital which is often used as a highly ornamented versal or initial letter. The illumination is original and usually in the style of 'English leaf' when the art was in its heyday. Some of the earlier pages owe more to the French filigree style as in the frontispiece.

Each five-year volume contains over one hundred pages. Owing to the cost of facsimile reproduction only about half of the walks in the first four volumes have been selected – ten with complete text and seven with a theme preface and overall map. Before the invention of printing in the late fifteenth century, spelling was not standardized so the text has not been corrected except on the pages which, because they were not illuminated, are set in type.

Each volume begins with a general preface all of which, for the sake of continuity, have been included. Among the appendices excluded is a so-called 'Itinerarium' based on the Roman Antonine Itinerary: a road book giving routes and distances between places on them. This serves as a summary of the walks in each volume – by ITER and number. On p125 is a single example of another appendix, 'Walkers' Wisden' and on p46 a commentary on both. Other appendices excluded are the five yearly review and bibliography. To give some idea of the sources of our inspiration we have mentioned a few of the more significant books and authors on the next page. The selection of material for this journal closes with a Prologue after the Preface to Volume 5. This serves paradoxically as an epilogue by introducing newcomers to our group and so providing a link with the present day.

Like Johnnie Walker we are still going strong. At the close of 1990 we have walked over 4,000 miles on 300 days thus doubling the figures shown on p125. We have recently completed Iter LXXV and are, so to speak, walking half-way through Volume 8 – even though Volume 6 is not quite completed. Where will it all end? Maybe like the way this Journal ends; as T S Eliot has written:

> And the end of all our exploring
> Will be to arrive where we started
> And know the place for the first time.

MCMXC

GLOSSARY

ACOUSTIC JARS (p85) – Large earthenware jars designed to improve speech and music quality by resonance.

AGGER (p19) – The embankment of a Roman road.

BEATUS PAGE (p45) – A highly ornamented page; the term is used here to describe pp34 and 35.

BRAUNCHE BRASS (p43) – The brass depicts the 'Peacock' feast of a former mayor of King's Lynn named Braunche.

CELURE (p63) – A panelled and decorated part of the roof above the rood and screen.

DOMINICAL LETTER (p27) – One of the letters A–G used year by year to denote the incidence of Sundays (Lord's Days).

LONG AND SHORT WORK (p25) – Arrangement of quoin stones alternately upright and horizontal.

LONG TOM COUNTRY MIXTURE (pp93 and 122) – Noisome heaps found in farmyards – sadly not so often today.

LYNCHETS (p27) – The remains on hillsides of early Iron Age cornlands caused by repeated ploughing.

MILECASTLE (p64 et seq) – Small forts, one Roman mile apart, manned by a patrol garrison.

MILLIA PASSUM (p68) – The Roman mile which was 1000 paces of a runner's stride of nearly five feet.

PIEDS POUDRÉS (p33) – 'Dusty feet', that is, of wayfarers, who could be tried by Courts of 'Pied-Powder' set up at fairs to settle disputes.

RINGELMAN (p121) – Number code to define the quality and strength of tea; 'Ringelman 8' is a good cup.

TURRETS (p64 et seq) – Two small signalling towers spaced evenly between each pair of milecastles.

VALLUM (p64 et seq) – Flat-bottomed ditch with mound on each side to prevent access to military area.

WEEPING CHANCEL (p57) – Out of line with nave and said to mark inclined head of Christ on the Cross.

WINKLE SHOOTER (p120) – Tweed hat without ear-flaps.

ACKNOWLEDGEMENTS

Over the years the confraternity of walkers has contributed in various ways towards 'A Book of Walks', a selection from which appears here as *The Wayfarers' Journal*. After the first walk in 1953 seven years elapsed before it was decided to begin the record upon the untimely death of Val (H A Valentine), who was one of the original four.

From the beginning Mick (M B Sellars), who shares our love of antiquities, old churches and pubs, has been diligent in supplying full details of church architecture and fittings in the absence of a descriptive pamphlet. He has always been prepared to provide a record of walks, in particular of those which Pat could not attend.

In the background during the early years was Bill Ward, who bound each volume in leather with gold tooling. In 1978, when he joined us on the road, he brought with him home-made pilgrim badges to wear in our hats. In 1983 he photocopied and bound in a single cover the first four volumes of 'A Book of Walks' so that each of us could have a copy.

The other Bill (W Adams) first joined us along with the late Father Cuthbert Smith in 1967. While the latter took on the heavy burden of catering for our spiritual needs – to such good effect that he was appointed our chaplain – Bill has been no less effective in providing for our material needs. Thus, tiring of our dilatory habits, he insisted on booking accommodation and on bringing supplies of tea, milk, sugar and biscuits.

The revered Father Cuthbert died aged eighty-two in 1981. In the course of a hundred miles of his limited spare time he revived in us the spirit of pilgrimage. We are pleased to welcome his recent successor, Father Pat Faughnan and look forward to many happy years in his company.

George (G Reynolds) deserted the river bank for the footpath in 1974. Despite an initial 'baptism' of pouring rain, he persevered and remains as enthusiastic as the rest of us.

Jack Coombs and Sam Weller, though not regular walkers, are honorary members of the confraternity and invariably attend our quarterly meetings. Sam Weller takes on the task of describing us all in more detail in the opening pages of Volume 5.

Among occasional walkers were Egg (H Eggleton) whom we met at King's Lynn on the Norfolk Walk, and Gerry (G A T Lilley) who came with us on Romney Marsh. Another former colleague is Jack Ellarby with whom we stayed for two nights on Exmoor.

The verse recalling our first walk to Canterbury in 1953 was written by the late Wilfred Sellars. We owe much to his inspiration and early encouragement. While Hilaire Belloc's book *The Old Road* guided us along the Pilgrims' Way, his preface to *The Four Men* epitomized our urge to record our walks and to re-enact that farrago in 1956. The extract from *The Four Men* is reproduced by permission of the Peters Fraser and Dunlop Group Ltd.

The 'golden sessions', when we have our feet up, are echoed by C S Lewis in *The Four Loves*. An extract from this book is included in the preface to Volume 2 by kind permission of Harper Collins Publishers.

In the preface to ITER VIII we refer to an article in *The Times* of 26 August 1959. The writer was Bernard Berry whose poem 'Turnip Field near Dinton' (p 17) was first published in *The Field*, 16 April 1959. The painting above it, by John Lloyd, is an impression of Stane Street near Gumber Corner. On Stane Street (ITER X) we used *Roman Ways in the Weald* by Ivan D Margary. His field workers called themselves 'Viatores', a name which we adopted for ourselves and have acknowledged elsewhere.

For much information about Hadrian's Wall we are indebted to *The Handbook to the Roman Wall* by J Collingwood Bruce first published in 1863. We drew from the twelfth edition, edited by Sir Ian Richmond (1965); we thank Charles Daniels MA, FSA (the present editor) for permission to use this source for the many inscriptions and other details in our account of the Wall.

For details about the Old Roads of Coulsdon (pp 104/5) we are grateful to The Bourne Society and their book *Coulsdon Downland Village* (1976) by Una Broadbent. The history of the Norbury Outpost Rambling Club was written by the late Fred Rice.

For our rendering of the New Canterbury Tales we have quoted or slightly amended a dozen lines from Nevill Coghill's translation of Chaucer's work into modern English with the permission of Penguin Books Ltd.

The Authors' Note ends with three lines from T S Eliot's 'Little Gidding' reproduced by kind permission of Faber and Faber London.

With the exception of those which resemble antique maps, the maps are based on Ordnance Survey maps with the permission of the Controller of HMSO © Crown Copyright.

We have made every effort to contact the owners of the copyright of all the information contained in this book, but if, for any reason any acknowledgements have been omitted, we ask those concerned to contact the publishers.

In April 1989 we met Douglas McCreath. He took an unexpected interest in 'A Book of Walks'; at the time we had no thought of publication but he did. We thank him for acting as our agent, for suggesting the title and writing the Introduction to this book.

Having 'walked out', as it were, on our wives and children so many times, we must acknowledge their unstinting support and co-operation over the years. Thirty years ago we wrote that we dedicated 'A Book of Walks' to our wives; we do so again with *The Wayfarers' Journal*.

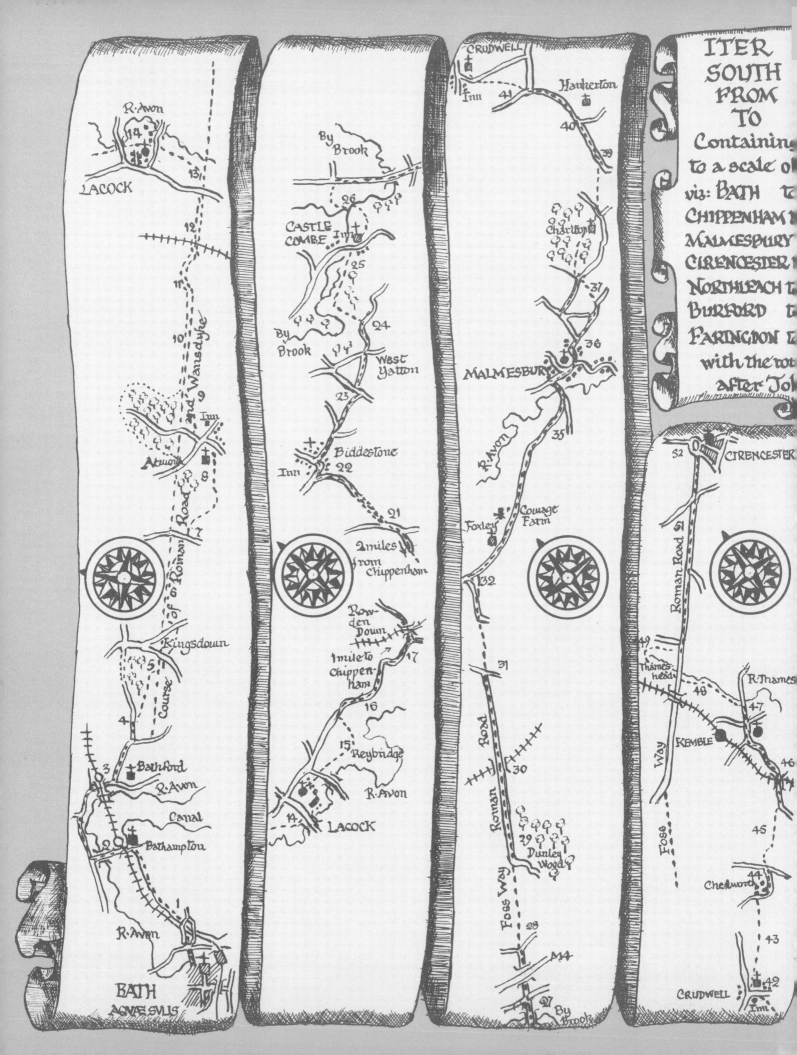